Plato's Metaphysics of Education

Plato's Metaphysics of Education

Samuel Scolnicov
The Hebrew University of Jerusalem

Routledge
London and New York

For Hanna, again

First published in 1988 by
Routledge
11 New Fetter Lane, London EC4P 4EE

Published in the USA by
Routledge
in association with Routledge, Chapman and Hall, Inc.
29 West 35th Street, New York, NY 10001

Set in 10/11pt Times by
BookEns, Saffron Walden, Essex
and printed in Great Britain by
T. J. Press (Padstow) Ltd. Padstow, Cornwall.

Library of Congress Cataloging in Publication Data
Scolnicov, Samuel.
　Plato's metaphysics of education/Samuel Scolnicov.
　p.　cm.
　Bibliography: p.
　Includes index.
　1. Plato—Contributions in education. 2. Education, Greek—
Philosophy.　I. Title.
LB85.P7S36　1988
370'.1—dc19　　88-11450

British Library Cataloguing in Publication Data also available

ISBN 0-415-01864-1

Contents

Preface

This is a book about how Plato developed his metaphysics with a view to supporting his deepest educational convictions. It leads from the reaction of Plato's Socrates against the ethical and epistemological relativism of the sophists, to Plato's mature conception of education as a profound transformation of the personality, and to his considerations about education as the development of reason, understood as a normative principle of order.

The factual points of Plato's theory of education have been dealt with abundantly and adequately, and I shall not rehearse them here. My main interest is in the relation of Plato's metaphysics to the epistemological, ethical and political aspects of his theory of education. Without unduly modernizing Plato, I shall try to show how his basic positions – even when they seem to us, on the face of them, most outlandish – bear directly and heavily on modern educational problems.

The book is primarily aimed at educationalists, philosophers and historians of philosophy, although each will find in it, so I hope, something different. No knowledge of Greek is assumed in the text, but some philological material is found in the notes, where deemed necessary or desirable. A general acquaintance is presupposed with at least those of Plato's dialogues discussed below. A basic bibliography is provided at the head of the notes to each chapter.

Acknowledgements

Earlier versions of Chapters 3 and 6 were published in *Scripta Classica Israelica*; a version of Chapter 6 was also published in *The College* (St John's College, Annapolis, MA). I thank the editors for their kind permission to use this material.

Friedrich Solmsen, Ernst Manasse, Abraham Edel and David Heyd read parts of the manuscript and commented on them in detail. I profited much from my discussions with them, and where I did not the fault is mine. The initial research for this book was carried out at the National Humanities Center in North Carolina, to whose first president, the late Charles Frankel, I owe a special debt. Israel Scheffler instigated all the stages of this book. Without him it might have never come about.

My thanks to Allan Tutle, the Librarian of the NHC, to Lea Metsch and to Hagar Rosen for helping me with the bibliography. Hagar Rosen also prepared the index.

References to classical works

Plato is referred to by dialogue, page number, page section and line number of the standard edition by Henricus Stephanus, Paris, 1578. Stephanus' page numbers appear in the margin of all modern editions and translations. The text assumed, except where otherwise indicated, is that of J. Burnet in the Oxford Classical Texts series, *Platonis Opera*, 5 vols., Oxford, Clarendon Press, 1900–07.

Aristotle is referred to, except where otherwise indicated, by title of work, book and chapter, where appropriate, then page, column and line of the standard edition by Immanuel Bekker, Berlin, Royal Prussian Academy, 2 vols., 1831–1870. Bekker's pagination appears in the margin of all modern editions and translations. The text assumed is that of W.D. Ross in his various editions of the principal works of Aristotle, Oxford, Clarendon Press.

Pre-socratic philosophers and the sophists are quoted by the number of the fragment in the sixth edition of Hermann Diels, *Die Fragmente der Vorsokratiker*, edited by Walther Kranz, 3 vols., Dublin and Zurich, Weidmann, 1951. Fragments believed by Diels and Kranz to be genuine *verbatim* quotations of the philosopher are referred to as, e.g., fr. 3 or fr. 3 DK. *Testimonia*, i.e. reports of later authors about the philosopher, but not direct quotations of his works, are put by Diels and Kranz in section A of the chapter dealing with the philosopher, and are accordingly referred to as, e.g., A 5.

Homer, Aristophanes, Thucydides, Xenophon, Isocrates and Plotinus are referred to by title of work, then, where relevant, book, chapter, and paragraph or line, according to the Oxford Classical Texts series.

Diogenes Laertius, Sextus Empiricus and Pausanias are referred to by title of work (if more than one extant, as in the case of Sextus Empiricus), then book, chapter and paragraph, according to the Loeb Classical Library edition, London, Heinemann.

CHAPTER 1

Introduction

One cannot hope to discuss Plato's philosophy of education without discussing also Socrates'. A neat separation between master and disciple is notoriously impossible. From our point of view, however, we are interested in the Socrates that influenced Plato, as Plato perceived him. We must then try and make some sort of distinction between the Socratic and the Platonic elements in Plato's dialogues (rather than between the historical and the literary Socrates), i.e. between Plato's portrait of Socrates and Plato's literary and philosophical extrapolation of Socrates' views as Plato understood them.[1]

The question is too complex to be dealt with in this introduction and goes well beyond the scope of this book. Very broadly, one can say that Plato's Socrates is that Socrates in the dialogues who is still innocent of the doctrine of the ideas, of Pythagoreanism and of eschatology. But the venerable distinction between the early 'Socratic' dialogues and the middle and late 'Platonic' dialogues has to be handled with care. In the end, the line between the Socratic and the Platonic must be drawn within the dialogues themselves. But it passes inside the dialogues, not between them. In some dialogues, such as the *Gorgias* or the *Theaetetus*, Socrates is a highly composite figure. Elements such as the distinction of dialectic from rhetoric in the *Gorgias* or the art of midwifery in the *Theaetetus* could be genuinely Socratic, but the Pythagorean influence and the interest in eschatology and epistemology are best understood as Platonic.[2] Nevertheless, as a rough guide, one could point to the final myth of the *Gorgias* and the second part of the *Meno* (from the introduction of the myth of recollection) as the nearest one can come to identifying a watershed between Plato's 'historical' Socrates and the Platonic Socrates, who is hardly more than a literary figure.[3]

There is also a difference in method between Plato's Socrates and the Platonic Socrates. Plato's Socrates is dialectical and elenctic. He will argue from the premises of his interlocutor and try to force him to go back on them. This means that elenctic dialogues have their scope circumscribed from the beginning by the positions put forward for discussion by Socrates' opponents. It is part of Socrates' educational approach that one has to come to see the shortcomings of one's opinions 'from within'.

It is in this sense that Socratic dialectic is intrinsically ironic. Socrates will always accept his opponent's view, for the sake of the argument, taking up from there. Socrates' attitude to his opponent's opinions is thus essentially ambivalent; he will accept a position in which he does not believe, only in order to disprove it.

The fundamental shortcoming of Socratic dialectic is plain; it is exclusively destructive. Socrates did have ethical convictions of his own, and his method implied some very strong underlying assumptions. But Socrates was prevented precisely by his method from arguing directly for his convictions. These could perhaps be summarized in the double assumption that – against sophistic relativism – there is a real difference between good and bad and between true and false.

Plato saw the limitations of Socratic elenchus. These are made clear towards the end of the *Gorgias*; Callicles, Polus and Gorgias, 'the three wisest among the Greeks of today' (527 B8–9), could not withstand Socrates' examination, and so Socrates is entitled to presume that his own view stands, as expressed in the concluding myth. But no real support has been given to it.

In the *Meno*, Plato proposes a new method, the method of hypothesis.[4] With his new method, Plato also implicitly puts forward a different conception of the task of philosophy. Philosophy is to provide the metaphysical foundation for the ethical and epistemological convictions which withstand elenchus, and specifically the Socratic convictions that doing evil is always wrong and that no one does evil willingly.

The absolute distinction between true and false, and good and bad, is to be assumed. The premises (in Plato's terminology, the *hupotheseis*) are sought which make such distinction possible, and the premises of these premises, until something is arrived at which is in no need of further support. Plato was well aware that metaphysical assumptions cannot be proved or deductively demonstrated. Their worth is in their power to provide a synoptical and unifying view, and to give support to a philosophical position whose alternative is considered untenable.[5]

Plato was thus led to consider firstly the kind of interest or utility Socrates was opposing to the sophists' utilitarian or individualistic concept of interest. He came to interpret it as non-empirical utility. Socrates had indeed talked of the care of one's soul as something opposed to simple utilitarianism, but he seems to have left it at that.

Plato was trying then to find out what reality must be like so that Socrates' moral and his own epistemological intuitions are vindicated. This implied the consideration of the nature of knowledge and its objects, the nature of the soul as the seat of cognition and desire and as the Socratic unity of the moral personality, and finally, the relation between subjectivity, as desire and personal conviction, and objectivity, as goodness and truth.

Socrates saw the individual as the object of education. Necessary conditions of the success of education were personal effort and personal commitment and conviction. But personal conviction had to lead to objectively valid truth and goodness. Socrates left Plato the question: How can the results of education both originate in each individual and yet be binding for all individuals? Plato saw the only solution in the assumption that the individual's real nature is not *in* him (in a sense to be explained below) and that his real desires and interests are transcendent to him, much as they are akin to him.

Education was then for Plato the leading of the individual from the empirical and particular to the purely intelligible. As with Socrates, the starting-point is always the world of everyday experience, from where the process of the development of reason has to start. But most people will not make it to full intelligibility, not because they will be kept behind but because, as a matter of fact, they will be incapable of continuing their education beyond a certain point. Platonic education is thus graded and selective; it is a gradual process of clarification of the irrational or semi-rational cognitive and emotional contents of the soul, leading to the realization of the objectivity of these contents, according to the capabilities of each individual. That most people cannot hope to be more than imperfectly educated is presumably a necessary consequence of such a view.

In the *Protagoras*, the *Gorgias* and the *Euthydemus*, Plato explores the opposition and the borderline between Socrates' and the sophists' conceptions of education. The *Meno* asks how Socrates' view of learning is possible, and the *Theaetetus*, a later dialogue, re-examines the nature of the objects of knowledge required by Plato's solution to the problem of Socratic learning. The *Phaedrus* and the *Symposium* consider desire and its object, and their relation to knowledge and reality. The *Republic* unfolds the whole process of education in its social context, from its irrational beginnings to the full apprehension of intelligible reality. Here Plato addresses himself not only to the attainment of full rationality and intelligibility but also to the semi-rational stages of education, through literature and art, and to the political management of a society most of whose members will not transcend subjectivity and particularism.

I have only occasionally referred to the earlier dialogues, in order not to tip the balance of the book to the Socratic side. At the other end, I have omitted a discussion of the *Laws*. With all its importance to Plato's theory, and his recommended practice, of education, the main philosophical foundations had already been laid in Plato's middle dialogues.

CHAPTER 2

The background and the challenge: sophistic education

In Plato's dialogue *Protagoras*, Hippocrates, a young man of good family, excitedly awakens Socrates before dawn, and urges him that they go and see Protagoras, the sophist, who had just arrived in town.[1] Although Socrates seems nonplussed and restrains Hippocrates from rushing to Protagoras' lodgings at that early hour, yet the sophist's visit to Athens was some reason for excitement.

The sophists brought about a revolution in Greek education. Until the middle of the fifth century BC, education had been traditional, and human and political excellence[2] were considered primarily a matter of birth and family, not of training and formal education. But by the middle of the fifth century traditional education and the customary ways of managing political life in Greece, and especially in Athens, were proving inadequate. The rise of democracy posed the question of the education of political leadership. True, in Athens political leaders still continued to come, for some time, from the wealthy aristocratic families – a phenomenon not unknown in our own times. But statemanship was now considered an art to be mastered, and the sophists provided for the need for instructors in that art. The sophists maintained, for the first time in Western history, that family education ought to be supplemented and completed by professional educators.[3] The ideal of the well-educated person from now on rivalled that of the nobleman.

The sophists held out the promise of civic and political excellence for all – or at least for those who could pay. Some of them announced themselves educators in political excellence and individual success. In Athens, civic upbringing had traditionally occurred by direct participation in the city's life. The education of the youth was considered the concern of all citizens alike. Political excellence was not thought of as a technique to be learned, but as a mode of life which the young absorbed through living in society. To be educated was not on the same footing as having a trade or having mastered an art. Thus, it is not strange that the sophists, coming from outside Athens, unable to participate actively in her political life yet influencing it to a great extent, were looked upon with a mixture of admiration and distrust.

Their educational outlook was eminently pragmatic. In political life absolute theoretical truth is irrelevant: it is success that counts. In stressing success, the sophists were continuing and reinforcing one main strand of the Homeric tradition. Manly excellence was, in Homer, military prowess, success in war and in the defence of one's household, and the skills which contributed to it. Closely related to such success, as both a prerequisite of it and justified by it, were the privileges of a high social position. Obviously, the notion of excellence was different for women and for the dependents of the household.[4] This aristocratic aspect of excellence is considerably weakened by the fifth century BC, especially in Athens. Out of it, however, arose various forms of ethical relativism.

At the same time, the sophists were reacting against the philosophy of nature that had developed in Ionia and in Greek Italy since the end of the seventh century BC. The outlandish claims of the earlier natural philosophers about the nature of reality had led to a complete dissociation of scientific, i.e. speculative, knowledge from the workaday opinions by which men live their lives. The older sophists did not negate this dissociation, but they gave it a new slant by shifting the interest from the speculative to the practical and the inductive. For them, the relevant questions were not those of truth and falsehood, but those of what is and what is not effective in this or that situation, of expediency, of know-how, of what are the best means to further one's own ends. Even Protagoras' essay on Truth and Gorgias' treatise on What-is-not, speculative as they may be, served them as epistemological foundations for practical positions.[5]

It is not that the natural philosophers of the sixth century BC were not interested in human and social affairs. Much on the contrary, some of them were reputed to have drawn constitutions for Greek cities and to have taken an active part in politics. The Pythagoreans may even have tried to integrate their philosophical speculation and their political activity. But the sophists reversed the priorities and came to see the justification of speculative thinking in its relevance to human concerns.

There is thus no point in teaching others, if by 'teaching' one means conveying the truth about the way things are. Rather, one seeks to convince, to persuade, to prevail, by psychological means more than on logical grounds; for in the world of action it is not the dispassionate logical arguments that carry the day, but – as in Parliament and in the court house – psychological motives and considerations. Sophistic education as a preparation for practical, and especially political, success dealt heavily in rhetoric, the instrument of persuasion and of public life. Some sophists also pursued other branches of knowledge, for the first time in a systematic manner; they inquired into the possibility of knowledge, into the foundations of society, into the sources of language and of religion, into grammar and poetry criticism, and in a lesser degree pursued also mathematics, astronomy and music.

Controversy about what knowledge is of most worth was rife in fifth-century Athens. While Hippias of Elis' curriculum, for example, was truly encyclopedic, Protagoras would concentrate on the arts of speaking and of government, and Gorgias would deny teaching anything but rhetoric. For all, however, the motivation remained always practical. Knowledge was considered desirable not so much for itself, for the satisfaction of one's curiosity about the universe, as for its practical results, for its efficacy in furthering one's aims.

Protagoras of Abdera is reputed to have been the first Greek to teach private and political excellence for a fee – and a high one at that. Given his philosophical position, this may seem odd. His *Truth* opened with the words: 'Of all things man is the measure: of those that are that they are; of those that are not that they are not.'[6] This was a new and disturbing concept of truth. The criterion of truth is not what is the case objectively, independently of the observer, but, much on the contrary, truth is dependent on each man's subjective perception. Man is not only the criterion of the efficacy of things, of their value as means for ends, but also of their very being or not being so-and-so.

For Protagoras, there is no objective reality which appears to some in this way and to some in a different way. There are no 'primary' qualities which, on being perceived by different subjects, appear as so many 'secondary' qualities. For Democritus, the atomist, individual differences between perceptions of the same object would be caused by differences in the perceiving organism, while the perceived object itself has a reality of its own, viz. atoms and void. Democritus was probably reacting to Protagoras' thorough-going subjectivism. Protagoras' claim seems to have been something like the following: Beyond what appears to me or to you, there is no common independent reality. The object *is* its appearances. There is no object which appears to different people differently, but the object is for each person what it appears to be for him, and there is no advantage to one appearance over another. The question, But what is the object itself independent of the observer? is meaningless.[7]

Protagoras could, thus, negate the possibility of contradiction: 'On every issue there are two arguments opposed to each other.' But the opposed arguments or propositions (*logoi*) are not related to each other as truth and falsehood, for they are not mutually exclusive. Both are true, for neither presents the issue or the thing as it is in itself, but as it appears, i.e. as it is, for me or for you.[8]

It is, therefore, impossible to teach, i.e. to convey objective truths. But it is possible to persuade. Indeed, Protagoras used to promise 'to make the weaker argument stronger'.[9] Of course, by calling one argument 'weaker' and the other 'stronger', Protagoras could not intend to evaluate the intrinsic, objective validity of each argument, for he denied any such validity apart from what appeared to me or to you. He seemed rather to be applying these terms to the psychological efficacy of the arguments. The stronger argument is the persuasive argument, the argument which carries conviction. The question of logical validity is, from this point of view, irrelevant. Protagoras promised to turn the less persuasive argument into the more persuasive – a promise consistent with his criterion of truth and one on which he could certainly make good.

Nevertheless, Protagoras did see himself as a teacher and educator, whose art was to bring up men to personal and political excellence, so that they might best manage their own household and the state's affairs.[10] This seems paradoxical; if the truth is to each person as it appears to him, what is the point of education?

We do not know what Protagoras himself had to say on this, but Plato provides him with an answer perfectly consistent with the Protagorean line[11]; the wise man is not he who can change 'false' perceptions into 'true' ones. This cannot be, for what each man perceives is so for him so long as he so perceives it. Rather, the wise man is he who is able to change the man to whom certain things seemed bad (and therefore were bad for him), so that these things will seem to him good and thus be good for him. The educator's work is analogous to the doctor's; the doctor does not pass judgment on the truth of the patient's perceptions. Rather, he tries to change the patient so that his perceptions will be changed too. Moreover, when the change is completed, the patient himself will prefer his new state to that in which he was before the treatment. But he will not deem his state truer. Thus, education does not correct mistaken judgments, but changes undesirable states into desirable ones.

Protagoras' doctrine arguably is the ancestor of modern educational theories which see in mental health or in social adjustment the aim of education (or one of the chief aims of education). The essential argument against the Protagorean position has not changed since Plato; the choice of a 'normal' or 'preferred' as against an 'abnormal' state can be made only on some soundly-based conception of human nature. This is incompatible with a subjectivism which puts all perceptions and valuations on an equal footing. Thus, in Plato's eyes, a theory of education needs a philosophy of human nature and of nature in general.[12]

Protagoras' views on political excellence are more complex. Plato's presentation of them in the *Protagoras* seems fairly reliable. Justice and reverence are a necessary condition of all social and political life. By justice Protagoras seems to have meant an accepted principle of distribution, as opposed to purely subjective interest.

There must be thus a recognition (even if only tacit) that there are just, as distinct from unjust, modes of distribution of resources and privileges. This recognition, however, is not sufficient. There must also be a motive for a person behaving justly, i.e. there must be a motive for the acceptance of the precedence of the objective principle of distribution over the subjective interest.[13] The alternative would be to acknowledge the existence of a recognized principle and the opposition between it and subjective interest, but to deny that one should act on it. (This was, in fact, Callicles' position in Plato's *Gorgias*.)

Such a motive is reverence or shame (*aidos*), the fundamental acknowledgment that man is a social animal, that he is unable to shut himself off completely from society. Reverence or shame is the individual's acknowledgment of his inability to disregard systematically and in all cases the restrictions imposed by society on behaviour which is exclusively self-oriented. For Protagoras, a sense of reverence and justice is innate in man, but it is only a presupposition of political life and of social and political education. Therefore, political excellence can and must be taught and developed.[14]

Gorgias of Leontini was better known as an orator and teacher of rhetoric. Unlike Protagoras, he did not propose to teach political excellence, nor did he engage in other disciplines, as did other sophists. Whereas all sophists taught rhetoric, Gorgias taught it exclusively, and with great success. Indeed, it is hard to underestimate his influence on later Greek and Roman oratoric art.

There was in Gorgias' rhetoric an important element of entertainment and aestheticism.[15] But the main avowed object of Gorgias' oratory was persuasion, not entertainment. Rhetoric is the general art of persuasion, which makes all into willing slaves. It has no subject of its own, but deals with all subjects, although Gorgias seems to have mentioned in this context especially legal and political matters. Irrational elements played an important role in the art of persuasion, such as arousal of emotions and of laughter, and peculiarities of style.[16]

The philosophical underpinning of his position was given in his little treatise *On Nature or On What There Is Not*, which reached us in two somewhat different summaries. This treatise may have been a parody of earlier metaphysical speculation, but, at least in the parts which interest us, Gorgias' intentions appear to be perfectly serious.[17]

The work opens with the statement that nothing is, and goes on to 'prove' this statement by means of an involved argument which we do not have to follow here. But, Gorgias continues, even if there were anything, it would be unknowable, for phenomenologically, from the point of view of the subject, there is no difference between true and false cognition. All that is given to us are our perceptions, and by examining their internal structure we cannot tell which correspond to independent realities and which do not; a perception of a chariot running over the sea or of a flying man can be as clear and distinct as any 'true' perception about which we have no qualms in referring to an independent reality.

Even if reality could be apprehended, continues Gorgias, it could not be communicated to another person, for speech transmits sounds, not that which is in fact apprehended, say the colour yellow, and which is what I want to communicate. Gorgias asks for the nexus of the sign to the signified and does not find it. One can communicate words: one cannot communicate things or meanings.[18] Words are severed from the world and there is no way in which they can have a denotation, either because there is nothing to denote, or because any relation between thought (or speech) and reality is impossible. Thus, the subject's assent to, or dissent from, a proposition are not related to his grasp of the relevant state of affairs. The determining factor in the assent or the dissent is persuasion alone, on purely psychological grounds.

We cannot deal with what is and we cannot know it; we can communicate words which do not enunciate knowledge of any sort. All we are left with is a technique of the use of words – rhetoric. Being dissociated from any object, rhetoric is absolutely general and completely indifferent to content or truth. Gorgias' rhetorical exercises, like the *Encomium of Helen* or the *Defence of Palamedes*, do not attempt to put forward a position which seemed to him truer or preferable on some criterion. They are rather virtuoso displays in the art of oratory. However, behind this show of virtuosity there was a deep scepticism about the possibility of knowledge. As a consequence of such scepticism, rhetoric was seen as the prototype of a technique to be mastered without regard for its ends. This extreme conclusion is presented and criticized in Plato's *Gorgias*.[19]

Hippias of Elis was described by Xenophon, his contemporary, as a polymath.[20] He taught a wide variety of topics, having been apparently the first to insist upon the educational importance of the subjects that were later to become the quadrivium: arithmetic, geometry, astronomy and 'music' (i.e. acoustics). But his fare included also grammar, mythology, genealogy and chronology, anthropology and history. He is said to have discoursed also on painting and sculpture, and, as most sophists, taught rhetoric and practical poetry evaluation – the latter, as usual, rather for its moral content than for its aesthetic form. Hippias was renowned for his prodigious memory and by the mnemonic techniques he developed and taught.

He may also possibly have made some original contribution to mathematics. More than any other sophist, his was the epitome of an encyclopedic education.[21]

It is not surprising that the question of the justification of social institutions should have been ardently debated in fifth-century Athens. The story has been told many times and there is no need to go into details. The controversy ranged over a variety of topics; morals and education, law and political constitutions, language and religion. Most conspicuously the debates focused on whether justice and human excellence had any foundation in nature or whether they were, in their essential feature, merely conventional. In particular, it would seem that if human and social excellence was essentially inborn, it would not be, in an important sense, teachable, although it might, of course, still be developed from an initial ability or capacity. On the other hand, if it was socially conditioned, it would be primarily a product of education, an art to be learned, with no preconditions which could not, in principle, be attained by everyone, or done away with altogether. (This distinction was not always so clear cut; Protagoras, as we saw, held a sort of compound position.)

But a clear contrast between the positive law of the land and human nature is drawn only in the fifth century BC by Antiphon. Justice consists in not transgressing the customs of the city in which one enjoys citizenship. In particular one should beware of breaking the law when there are witnesses, although when no witnesses are present one is free to act in one's best interest.[22]

Antiphon saw that an understanding of the psychology of the individual as the proper foundation of social and political well-being is necessary for any political theory. In this context too we should appreciate his occasional pronouncements on education. First among human activities is education. A good education is like a good seed planted in a young body, which will withstand rain or drought. Hence the importance of discipline as formative of character. Likewise, the child's character will become similar to the character of the person with whom he spends most of his time.[23]

Antiphon's views are close to those of the advocates of the so-called social contract theory, such as Protagoras, whose views have been discussed above, and Glaucon, Plato's brother (in *Republic* II, no doubt representing Plato's own improvement on fifth-century views). As Antiphon and Hippias of Elis, Glaucon too sees no natural foundation for the social institutions and the laws of the state. Self-interest is natural to man and social organization is opposed to self-interest. However, self-interest without social organization leads to insecurity. Therefore, society is a compromise between man's nature and his shortcomings. If he could, he would dispense with it.

Judging from Aristotle's criticism of his style, Lycophron seems to have been a pupil of Gorgias. He considered the law 'a mutual guarantee of justice' between the citizens. Aristotle contrasts his view with the traditional educational role of the law. Hippodamus, said to have been the inventor of city-planning and the first to research into the forms of government, reduced the laws to three types only, dealing with insult, injury and homicide.[24]

Some aspects of the pragmatic view of education characteristic of the sophists were to be developed later by Isocrates, Plato's contemporary. However, it would be misleading to understand the opposition of the conceptions of education of Plato and Isocrates exclusively in terms of Socrates' attack on the sophists.[25] Isocrates is perhaps better seen as the father of the literary tradition in Western education, of an education based on the word as an instrument for the formation of the character and for political action, with little more than lip-service to conventional morality. Such an education was to flourish in Rome and in the humanism, and its influence is felt to this day. Plato would centre his education for character and action on scientific and philosophical knowledge.[26]

Himself a pupil of Gorgias, Isocrates set up his school with the express purpose of producing teachers of rhetoric, informed debaters capable of doing reasonably well in any discussion, and, in general, educated men of culture. Especially, his students were trained for participation in public affairs. Isocrates' curriculum included gymnastics, grammar, the study of the poets, the historians (Herodotus and Thucydides) and the philosophers, as well as some mathematics, and finally eristic or dialectic, the art of debate. His main concern was, of course, with rhetoric, to which alone, he thought, the name 'philosophy' was appropriate, for nothing should be called philosophy which is no help to us in the present in our speech or in our action.[27]

Astronomy and geometry he considered a gymanstic of the mind. They are useful, but should not be indulged in for too long. They do no more than increase one's aptitude for mastering greater and more serious studies. Man cannot attain such science that will enable him to know what has to be done and what has to be said. The wise man is he who has an intuitive grasp of the complexity of human affairs and can arrive by conjecture or opinion at the best course of action.[28]

Perhaps against Plato, and possibly misunderstanding him, Isocrates was convinced that 'the kind of art which can implant honesty and justice in depraved natures has never existed and does not exist'.[29] But, he went on, people can become better by trying to speak well and persuade their hearers. For, he says, it is inconceivable that one should compose a speech worthy of praise or honour on a petty subject. The good speaker will perforce 'select . . . those examples which are the most illustrious and the most edifying', and these will influence his own conduct. And, ultimately, words carry more conviction when spoken by a man of honourable character.[30] And should the man that had such an education turn out to be wicked, it is not the educator who is to blame; just as one would not fault the boxing instructor if his art is put to evil use by his pupil.[31]

Isocrates upheld current morality, and his argumentation is naive and unsophisticated. Philosophically, his importance is minimal, and he is no innovator. But perhaps precisely because of these facts, he apparently offers a rather faithful picture of the actual fifth-century Athenian view of education, and became an enduring influence on Western educational practice.[32]

CHAPTER 3

Socrates on the unity of the person

In that well-known passage of the *Apology*, after his conviction by the Athenian jury and before the penalty is imposed, Socrates gives his reasons for refusing to change his ways, even then: 'The unexamined life', he says, 'is not worth living for man.'[1] Few of his utterances describe him as well as this; if Socrates could ever be encapsulated in a few words, here he is.

The unexamined life is not worth living; such was Socrates' firm belief, because only constant inquiry can bring about the improvement of the soul. Before him, the Pythagoreans had already stressed the moral value of *theoria*, over and above its intellectual aspect: 'When asked what is [the purpose of human life], Pythagoras used to say: "To contemplate the heavens", and of himself he used to say that he contemplated the heavens.'[2] However, Socrates' interest was not in natural inquiry (although it might once have been, if Aristophanes and Plato are to be believed[3]). Unlike Pythagorean *theoria*, the immediate object of Socrates' intellectual activity was human action. His is not the contemplation of the ordered universe leading eventually to a corresponding order in the soul, but a consideration of human actions and their justifications. It is perhaps not devoid of significance that *theoria* in a technical sense makes its first appearance in the *Phaedo*. The Socrates of the early dialogues seems to prefer the philosophically more neutral *zetein* (search) or *skepsasthai* (inquire) to the Pythagorically-flavoured *theorein*.[4]

Like the sophists, his contemporaries, Socrates' bent was ethical, perhaps even narrowly ethical. His aims as well as theirs were practical; knowledge was ultimately for the sake of action and the good life. But while for the sophists inquiry had an instrumental, almost pragmatic, importance, for Socrates it had in itself moral value. Socrates not only inquired into human excellence; he saw this same inquiry itself as at least part of the excellence sought. However, Socrates' was not a romantic quest to be cherished regardless of its results. The dialectical search should eventually lead to the truth, and this truth is independent of the search for it. But this is not to say that the moral value of inquiry is derivative from the truth it leads to. Socrates was convinced that *arete* is *episteme*, virtue is knowledge, and knowledge, as Socrates understood it, cannot be dissociated from the reasons that support it.[5] In his eyes, knowledge was morally, and not only epistemically, superior to true but unsupported opinions, precisely in that he who has knowledge can given an account of it.

But how can inquiry have so deep a psychological power that it is able to bring about such a transformation of the soul, even to the point that *akrasia*, weakness of the will, becomes impossible? What is the conception of the soul that underlies such an intellectualistic view of its improvement?

For Socrates, the soul was nothing more than that by which we are good or bad and which becomes better by knowledge and worse by ignorance.[6] He seemed not to have held any explicit metaphysical doctrine about the soul, though its improvement was his foremost preoccupation. And as in this case what he said is of little help, if we wish to grasp some of his meaning we have to look into what he did. An inspection of Socrates' practices in the earlier Platonic dialogues will show that there are three main demands which he makes of his interlocutors: the demand that answers be given out of personal conviction; the demand for consistency; and the demand for definitions.

The first demand, that the respondent speak out of commitment for his opinions, means among other things that one is held personally responsible for them, and no opinion is to be maintained solely on trust or authority. Authority in itself is not enough, be it the authority of the rich, the noble, even the authority of the sage, or, *a fortiori*, the authority of the many, in the form of tradition, common sense, or democratic vote.[7] The Socratic elenchus is not an examination of disembodied opinions, but of beliefs which are the interlocutor's own, at least for the time being.

The second demand, the demand for consistency, means that a man is responsible for the coherence, or at least the consistency, of his various opinions, and he is enjoined to check each and every one of them (but not all of them at once) for its compatibility or otherwise with his other relevant opinions.

The third demand, the demand for definitions, provides Socrates with a powerful logical tool with which to lay bare the inconsistencies in one's body of opinions and, more importantly, in one's actions. As we shall see, the demand for definitions is the guarantee of the objective value of the consistency and the conviction sought by Socrates.

It seems that Socrates sought in the words and actions of each and every one of his interlocutors a certain unity, a 'harmony' as he put it. This harmony is expressed in the avoidance of contradiction in word and deed, and this is the good for man.[8] But a merely 'external' harmony is not sufficient. It is necessary not only that the opinions examined be compatible with each other, but also, perhaps chiefly, that they be 'one's own'.

Clearly, the mere fact that I can formulate a certain opinion in words does not make that opinion mine. For what does it mean to say that an opinion is mine? Of course, this question cannot be answered by appeal to the established criteria, by which I say this house is mine, or this hand is mine, or this coat is mine, seeing that I have no title of ownership over my opinions, nor are they attached to me as a part of my body, nor do I have over them any claim of possession in the usual sense. Nevertheless, we seem to understand Socrates' satisfaction when someone answers him 'according to his own opinion' or 'as it seems to him', and so does Meno when he agrees that the boy's answers were indeed 'his'.[9]

From what has been said up to now about Socrates' demands, it appears that he thought that an opinion becomes 'mine' – for opinions can 'become' one's own – as opposed to an opinion 'of somebody else' which I merely quote, if it fulfills at least two conditions, each of them necessary and both jointly sufficient:

(a) I am convinced of its truth; and
(b) I can integrate it without contradiction with my other opinions.[10]

And, conversely, to be 'myself' is, to a great extent, to display a certain coherence, or at least a certain consistency, of beliefs earnestly held. (For Socrates, as for Plato, the basic logical relation is the relation of contradiction – or of lack of contradiction – and not the stronger relation of coherence.[11])

The same is true of one's actions, and of the relation of one's actions to one's opinions. The lack of such consistency in one's actions and beliefs is thought, in extreme cases, to be pathological. And indeed Plato in the *Republic* and Socrates in the *Gorgias* (in so far as the *Gorgias* depicts the 'historical' Socrates) both speak of the inability to unify the personality, i.e. the inability to integrate one's actions and opinions, as mental illness.[12]

The idea of a unified personality, which is responsible for one's action, was, in the fifth century BC, a novelty. In archaic thought such a unity is not self-evident. Each action, in so far as it is felt as needing explanation, is explained on its own. More often than not, one of the gods or a *daimon* is involved in important actions, although the concomitant responsibility of the agent is not thereby excluded.[13] It is only with Heraclitus, towards the end of the sixth century BC, that a notion of personal responsibility based upon the unity of the moral agent is evolved. 'Character is a man's *daimon*', he says.[14] A man's actions are not to be traced back to a *daimon* or to fate, but to his *ethos*, to the totality of his habits and ways of acting.[15]

For Socrates, the whole of one's actions and one's cognition becomes the focus of moral interest. By stressing the intellectual element in the unified personality, Socrates picks up the deliberation based on knowledge as the morally relevant aspect of the action. The moral agent is no longer considered merely as a unity of habits and ways of acting, but chiefly as a unity of thought and of action following upon thought.

Socrates' chief philosophical and educational interest seems to have been not in the finished act, but in the reasoned consideration, in the impact of thought upon action. Greek tragedy had already emphasized, shortly before Socrates, the intellectual element in human action, pitching conflicting points of view against each other on stage. But apparently it was Socrates who strictly made the rightness of one's action dependent upon deliberation based on knowledge.[16] For him, intellectual activity was for the sake of right action, but the rightness of the action was not independent of the intellectual activity involved in it. The distinction is a fine one, and Xenophon, for one, does not always seem to grasp it. In this respect, the comparison of *Memorabilia* I 4 18–19 with the conclusion of the *Euthyphro* is rewarding.

By the improvement of one's soul, then, Socrates meant making one's self better by means of constant examination of one's opinions and of the opinions of others. But the value of self-examination is not in the rightness of the moral opinions which, so one hopes, are achieved by such a process. Right but disjointed beliefs about courage or justice do the soul little good. It is their integration into a consistent pattern of reasoning and justification that constitutes the soul's well-being.[17] Such an integration can only be arrived at by means of conscious reflection on one's beliefs. This reflection, by creating the integration of one's system of opinions (and actions), also creates, in itself, the integration of the soul.

It is true that the opinions that Socrates sets out to examine were, on the whole, opinions about morals or, more exactly, about matters of conduct. But Socrates' momentous innovation seems to have been the emphasis he put on the moral importance of duly justified deliberation, as opposed to the value of right moral opinions not necessarily supported by reasoning. Of course, sound moral arguments imply true moral opinions, but not conversely. And Socrates obviously recognized that a valid argument is at least a step towards a true and reasoned conclusion, whereas an unsupported opinion, no matter if true or false, is an obstacle in the way of intellectual and moral improvement. This is one of the reasons why so many beliefs are overthrown by Socrates in one dialogue, which turn out in another to be not so far from the truth. But disconnected from their reasons, they have no great value.

Socrates saw himself as an educator. But, unlike the sophists, he did not consider himself a teacher; he professed to know nothing, hence to teach nothing.[18] The mission on which he believed Apollo had sent him was to examine each and every moral opinion, his fellow-citizens' as well as his own.[19] But Socrates did not examine his fellows' opinions for truth or falsity. This, in fact, he could not do, since in order to do it he would have needed a criterion for distinguishing true opinions from false ones. And it was just such a criterion which he claimed not to possess, save perhaps in some matters of small consequence, as when he found that artisans were knowledgeable about their crafts.[20]

Instead, Socrates looked for inconsistencies. His quest took two forms: on the one hand, he searched for possible contradictions in one's opinions, including the conclusions one is prepared to admit that follow from them, and between these and one's body of beliefs; on the other hand, he demanded a general and abstract configuration (*eidos*) which would justify one's use of the same word ('piety', 'courage', 'friendship') to describe apparently dissimilar situations as well as one's refusal to use the same word in cases which *prima facie* look pretty much alike.

However, the Socratic procedure should not be construed as pure conceptual analysis.[21] Even when Socrates does appeal to linguistic intuitions (and he does it quite often), he implies in them moral judgments too. Therefore – and no doubt also, but not exclusively, because of the range of concepts involved – Socrates' inquiries would have direct moral implications. How far this is true also of conceptual analysis is no longer a burning question. In any case, Socrates' inquiries had a much more obvious stake in morals than is sometimes conceded.

'Socrates asked, but never answered', said Aristotle, 'for he professed not to know.'[22] In the typical case, Socrates engaged his interlocutor in elenchus. By counter-examples, or by more elaborate indirect refutations, Socrates would force upon the respondent the realization of his ignorance. Admission of ignorance is a prerequisite to learning, but it is painful, and neither easily nor, in most cases, willingly arrived at. Thus, the elenchus is not only a logical and intellectual process, but also, if successful, a deep emotional transformation.[23]

Rather than a declaration of dogmatic scepticism, a blanket denial of the possibility of knowledge, Socrates' profession of ignorance was a radical openness to constant re-examination. No question was ever definitively closed, no opinion beyond doubt. If agreement was reached a while ago on a formulation which seemed then satisfactory, even such an agreement was not enough; for the conclusion to hold its value 'it must seem to us right not only a while ago, but also now and in the future'.[24] And although, in most of the cases, it is Socrates who conducts the conversation, his own opinions are also examined, for if his opponent is in the right, Socrates must be in the wrong.

There is indeed, in the Socratic demand for personal conviction, a marked Protagorean element. It was Protagoras who insisted on personal conviction as an inalienable criterion of truth. If the wind blows cold to me, it *is* cold to me, and I alone am entitled to judge its being so or not so, in so far as my own sensations are concerned. For Protagoras, this meant that the very being of things is always referred to a percipient (but not totally dependent on him); to be (so-and-so) is to be (so-and-so) for someone. But this is no Berkeleyan idealism: things are not ideas in a mind; they are, but they are for each man what they seem to him. Protagoras is more radical than Bishop Berkeley; man is the measure of all things and there is no God, whose mind can serve as the common measure of all ideas. The wind is cold (to me) and warm (to you), and this is all there is to it, with no possible compromise. Personal conviction, through sensation, intuition or persuasion, is the ultimate judge, and there is no appeal against its verdicts. The assent to, or the dissent from, any proposition rests ultimately on private grounds. The fact that the wind is cold to me (or warm to you) cannot be reduced to anything more basic. Such seems to have been Protagoras' position, at least as Plato understood him.

In this context, it is instructive to consider the central role played by contradiction in the thought of Socrates and of Protagoras, and their conflicting views on it. For Protagoras,[25] contradiction is an impossibility. Of course, 'p is true' and 'p is false' are contradictories. But Protagoras would consider these statements as elliptic statements which should be completed by a reference to the persons for whom p is true or false. And then, indeed, 'p is true for Jack' and 'p is false for Jill' or, in a more extreme formulation, 'p is true for Jack at time t_1' and 'p is false for Jack at time t_2', are not contradictories. By contrast, for Socrates, contradiction is the heart of the elenchus. Not only is contradiction possible for the same person over time, but it should be avoided at all times. Moreover, even inter-personal agreement is to be sought, although such agreement is not always within reach, nor, when reached, is it a guarantee of truth.

Such inter-personal agreement, if it is genuine and not a matter of shallow courtesy or shame, is, *prima facie*, an index (but not a guarantee) of the success of the inquiry into truth. Socrates stressed time and again that he wanted to secure only his interlocutor's admission to the proposition under investigation. He will not accept appeals to authority, he will not count heads, he will only grudgingly acknowledge agreements for the sake of the argument. He will always prefer a response which has his interlocutor's conviction, even if it cannot withstand criticism, to one that is probably sound, but uncritically borrowed. Nevertheless, Socrates was prepared to consider opinions quoted from poets, dreams, prophecies and the like, as long as one was prepared to examine them in earnest instead of relying on the authority of the source.

On the other hand, Socrates did not think that real agreement between the partners in the dialogue could arise out of rhetorical persuasion alone. Socrates expected his interlocutor to agree or to disagree with him on the strength of his own grasp of the state of affairs. It is true that quite often he would mislead his interlocutor and play on him eristic tricks. But, at least as Plato saw it, Socrates' purpose seems to have been for the most part[26] therapeutic; to entangle his interlocutor in contradictions in order to force upon him the recognition that his opinions are confused and only partly justified, if at all.

Socrates believed, unlike Protagoras, that there is a real difference between true and false, and between sound and unsound. He further believed that this difference becomes clear to one's mind on careful inspection of the propositions and arguments involved, if only one could be relieved of one's confused or irrelevant notions. The aim of the elenchus is to free a person from the opinions which are not 'his' in the strict, Socratic sense, i.e. those opinions uncritically accepted and therefore, in the typical case, not integrated, or straightforwardly incompatible, with one another. And once such a liberation has been achieved, so Socrates seems to have believed, the person will reach, of himself and almost against his will, that harmony which Socrates described to Polus and to Callicles.

However, mere coherence, let alone consistency, is not a sufficient guarantee of objective validity. That guarantee of the objective validity of personal and inter-personal consistency Socrates found in the *eidos* and in definition. It is the *eidos* that brings together the different objects or actions and presents them as variations of the same essential configuration. The definition circumscribes the *eidos*, being applicable to all relevant cases and only to the relevant cases. It guarantees the consistency of the use of the common name in all these cases and only in these cases, because it is a real definition answering to the *ti esti*, the 'what-is' question, and not a nominal definition which is merely a matter of convenience. Such a position does not imply, of course, a doctrine of ideas, like that in the *Phaedo* and in the *Republic*, but only a demand for a real object of definition, irrespective of its ontological status *vis-à-vis* the individual. Hence, Socrates' demand for definitions complements his demands for personal conviction and for consistency.

Thus, the Socratic elenchus, certainly in intention but perhaps also in practice, was not wholly negative. There was in it also that aspect which Socrates called *maieutike*, midwifery.[27] Ideally, the Socratic elenchus should clear the way for the development of true personal knowledge, stimulate that knowledge and build through it the intellectual and moral personality. But it is arguably no coincidence that the best examples of maieutical success are the geometry lesson in the *Meno*, the protreptic interludes with Clinias in the *Euthydemus* and the conversation with Theaetetus in the dialogue called after him – none of them in the early dialogues, which presumably portray a Socrates with a minimum of Platonic re-interpretation. As a rule, Socrates' attempts are not crowned with such success. In fact, the great majority of them ends in failure – at least in Plato's view; Xenophon gives us a sunnier picture of Socrates' endeavours.

Nevertheless, Socrates can do no more than bring his partners to the brink of the recognition of reasoned truth. Personal conviction remains an indispensable – but by no means sufficient – requisite of knowledge. It is the great irony of the Socratic dialogue that, even when Socrates holds an opinion which he believes to be true and well-supported (and sometimes it can be very difficult to decide whether this is the case) – even then he can only point at it indirectly, by way of negation.

But Socrates' irony was not a dissembling mask which he could remove at will. Behind it there was no secret to be revealed only to the initiated who successfully underwent the trial of the elenchus. Because knowledge can only be attained by personal effort, Socrates could not 'hand it down', but only hint at it by way of understatement.[28] And when his maieutic efforts failed, of necessity he had to let his interlocutor go – even if this meant, by Socrates' own standards, his moral perdition.

If Socrates' failure was, as is sometimes held against him,[29] a failure of love, still Socrates was inexorably led to it by his own philosophy. There is in this philosophy only one way to the salvation of the soul: the constant striving for consistency in one's actions and beliefs, to be achieved by personal effort. This is a long and hard way, and Socrates could point to it, but he could offer no shortcuts, for there are none. Right opinions in themselves do not add up to a unified and harmonic personality. Such a personality can arise only in the process of self-examination and cannot be separated from it.

CHAPTER 4

Education, teaching and training: *Protagoras*

In the *Protagoras*, for the first time in the Platonic corpus,[1] Socrates squarely confronts the sophistic notion of education. In the small 'Socratic' dialogues, Socrates' educational approach is exhibited more often than discussed, but we can discern some of its leading assumptions as they show through the examinations of the several virtues, taken in isolation. Indeed, it becomes apparent as we read the *Laches*, the *Lysis*, the *Charmides*, the *Euthyphro*, that courage, friendship, self-control and piety are each virtually identified with the totality of human excellence and put on a strictly intellectual base, if not in fact completely reduced to knowledge itself. Education, or the fostering of human excellence, emerges gradually in those little dialogues as the development of human reason.

But it is only in the *Protagoras* that the problem is presented in a general form. Is human and civic excellence knowledge? Can it be taught? Who are its teachers? What are the aims and what are the justifications of promoting human excellence in the young? In this dialogue Socrates engages the sophists directly, and the greatest of them all, Protagoras, on the ground which they declared their own – the education of men. Plato's question is: Can the sophists educate?

From an educational point of view, the main dividing issue between Socrates on the one hand and Protagoras and the sophists in general on the other is immediately delineated in the beginning of the dialogue – the role of knowledge in education. And although there are differences between Protagoras and Hippias (and Prodicus) on this point – at least before the last part of the dialogue – yet Socrates' criticism is aimed at all of them, by implication if not explicitly.

Already in the frame-story, Plato strikes the leading note: 'Must not what is wisest be considered finer[2]?' (309 C 11–12). As we shall see, this stands in contrast to Protagoras' view on the relation between knowledge and human excellence.

Young Hippocrates awakens Socrates before dawn and wants to see Protagoras, the sophist, immediately. It quickly becomes apparent that Hippocrates does not know what a sophist is, nor what he should expect from a sophistic education.[3] He acts on impulse, not on deliberation.[4] Socrates restrains him. What does Hippocrates expect from a sophistic education? Not, as in the case of the technical arts, to become a practitioner, i.e. not to make a living out of it. Rather, as Socrates suggests, Hippocrates comes to the sophist for the sake of his general education as a human being, not *epi techne* but *epi paideia*. Socrates immediately reinterprets this education for human excellence in general as 'the care of one's soul'. But in what consists this 'care of the soul'? Socrates implies that it cannot consist in the purely formal training of good speakers in whatever subject. On the contrary, he supposes that there can be no purely formal training in human excellence, but that such training or education must have a definite content (312 B).[5] On the other hand, in so far as sophistic education does have a content, such content is not imparted out of a consideration for its own educational value. The sophistic assumption is that knowledge is neutral, without intrinsic value, and its value comes only from the use to which it is put.[6] Socrates claims at 313 C–314 B that, on the contrary, knowledge itself – even in the weak sense of received belief – is not neutral, but has psychological and moral implications. In his words, it can be harmful or beneficial to the soul.

Protagoras certainly considers himself an educator. He is proud of having been the first to 'admit to being a sophist and educating men' (317 B). But he wants to dissociate himself carefully from Hippias and the others, who saw education as consisting of the teaching of technical subjects. Hippias' conception of education was encyclopedic; education for him was the learning of skills, arts and sciences.[7] His was, in a sense, an intellectualistic view of education. Plato chooses to make Protagoras emphasize this intellectual side of Hippias' approach; in describing Hippias' curriculum, Protagoras quotes disapprovingly arithmetic, astronomy, geometry and music.[8]

Protagoras denies, then, that the learning of skills and sciences has in itself any educational value. The other sophists, he says, in fact harm their pupils by teaching them those technical subjects against their will. But he, Protagoras, educates the young in human excellence, teaching them how best to care for their personal affairs and for the affairs of the state, and how to acquire political power (318 D–319 A).

Although Protagoras thinks such excellence to be teachable in some sense, yet he will not accept it as knowledge. His concept of knowledge seems to be the same as Hippias': technical instrumental knowledge, the sort of knowledge displayed in the arts and crafts, i.e. the knowledge of what means are appropriate to what ends. He would class the sciences together with the handicrafts.[9] Protagoras' myth makes the point that civic excellence, however, is not continuous with such knowledge. The arts and sciences of speech and language, building, garment-making and agriculture were, in the terms of the myth, given to men by Prometheus. They are sufficient for man's nurture, but they cannot form the basis of social and political organization. This is based not on knowledge, but on reverence and justice, whose psychological source is different from the source of the skill in arts and crafts. The myth tells us that reverence and justice were sent by Zeus, and are common to all mankind.[10] Protagoras willingly admits that justice, self-control and piety are 'almost the same', and they are the basis of political excellence (325 A).

Significantly, Protagoras does not include in his list two of the traditional Greek excellences, courage and wisdom or knowledge. Courage was probably omitted simply because Protagoras did not think it was a necessary condition of political association. At 349 D, Protagoras admits that courage is 'a part of excellence', although 'it is very different from the others'. The omission of wisdom is more important. Protagoras denies that excellence is knowledge (not distinguished here from wisdom), and sharply distinguishes between knowledge as mastery of skills and sciences, which has no moral or social value, and the moral and social excellences such as he listed. This is in keeping with Protagoras' distinction between what he does and what he does not teach.

This is why Socrates is so intent on proving, against Protagoras (and against apparent common sense), the unity of all virtues. The details of the argument have been worked many times over by commentators,[11] and they have no immediate bearing on our subject, except for its final section, the identification of courage and wisdom (349 E–350 C). Socrates starts this section by asking whether Protagoras thinks that the brave are the confident. Protagoras answers in the affirmative, describing courage as a lack of fear – as one would have expected. Socrates' second step is to gain Protagoras' emphatic assent to the proposition that all virtue is something fine (or noble, *kalon*), and it is not the case that some of it is fine and some of it not (349 E2–8). Socrates' elaboration on this point and Protagoras' repeated and enthusiastic endorsements are important, as we shall see presently. The third step is to establish, by a short induction from a series of examples,[12] that those who are more knowledgeable about certain matters are also more confident about those matters. Protagoras himself volunteers the generalization from Socrates' examples, without realizing that he thereby damages his own position. For, as Socrates goes on to point out, there are confident men who are not knowledgeable about the matters about which they are confident, even to the point of acting insensately. Obviously, these cannot be brave (350 B); for courage, being a virtue, is a fine thing, and foolish confidence is reprochable and cannot be a virtue (because all virtue is fine). By this argument, he says, courage will be knowledge.

But this conclusion is damaging to Protagoras' position only if Socrates' starting premise, 'The brave are the confident', is understood as a convertible proposition, i.e. if it is also granted that the confident are brave. And this, as Protagoras protests at 350 C, has not been accepted. Socrates, however, regards himself justified in considering Protagoras to be bound to accept – on his own premises – the identity of courage and confidence. For, if they are not identical, Protagoras must supply a *differentia* which singles out courage properly said from non-courageous confidence. This, for Socrates, can only be wisdom or knowledge, which Protagoras has denied as an excellence. Protagoras himself distinguishes courage and confidence differently: confidence is a matter of art and also of rage and madness; courage comes from one's nature and good education.

The distinction is not unlike his previous one; confidence is either wholly uncontrollable or it is indeed, as Socrates argued, dependent on art, i.e. on knowledge. In both cases it has no moral significance; courage is the result of the (non-intellectual) improvement of natural gifts, and as such it is worthy of praise.[13]

Socrates' final argument against Protagoras' separation of moral and intellectual virtue is the argument for the 'hedonic calculus', with which we shall deal later. But we should first conclude our discussion of Protagoras' great speech.

One might imagine that, on Protagorean grounds, human and political excellence both need not be taught, as it is possessed by all, and cannot be taught, as it is not knowledge. This would be consistent with a thoroughly democratic position. It is assumed, first, that political excellence is the ability to take wise decisions in matters of public interest, and it is presumed distinct from the expertise in setting out alternatives and implementing them. If this ability is inborn and universal, then all can equally participate in government, and distribution of offices by lot is justifiable. If, on the other hand, there is only a capacity that has to be developed by training or education, political office still is, in principle, open to all. A modified democratic view is then still possible, but not necessary. This seems to be Protagoras' position. Protagoras insists that human and political excellence can be taught. Reverence and justice, he explains, are only presuppositions of political excellence and of socio-political organization; they have to be properly nurtured and developed. Moreover, excellence is teachable, but not intellectually. Education in virtue is a matter of habituation, not of understanding. It is not like a technical subject in which one can be instructed, but it consists in the shaping of desirable behaviour.

Protagoras' little summary of Athenian education makes this clear (325 ff.). Nurse, mother, tutor and father inculcate in the child good habits, conditioning him into his social role and pointing out to him what is considered good or bad, according to the norms of his society. Later on, education is conducted by literary examples set for admonition and emulation. No understanding is implied, only ideal figures are held up for the youth to identify with. Similarly, music and gymnastics mould mind and body by training and imitation. And lastly, the laws themselves have an educative function,[14] setting a pattern of life to be followed by all citizens.

There is much in traditional Athenian education, as sketched by Protagoras in the dialogue, that Plato himself accepted. Early training, music and gymnastics are stressed in the *Republic* and especially in the *Laws*. Plato's recognition of the importance of the use of exemplary literary figures is at the bottom of his criticism of literature. However, if there is in these some educational value, they are certainly not the main road to human excellence, but only a preparation for the real education which is to come later, or a second best for those who are not capable of more.[15]

But here in the *Protagoras*, Plato attacks especially education through poetry – a favourite sophistic method. Socrates' exegetical exercise on Simonides (338 E–348 A) shows the futility of basing moral education exclusively on literature. Hermeneutics has no intrinsic limits. If one tries hard enough, any reading can be wrung out of a text, and the text – unlike a living person – cannot protest. In the absence of a theory of morals, literary pieces cannot serve as ethical authorities. Later, in the *Republic*, Plato himself will advocate the use of literature for the exemplification of moral ideals, but these moral ideals have to be independently established.

Punishment too is considered by Protagoras – perhaps for the first time in Western thought – as part of the educational process. It is not inflicted as vengeance or retribution, but 'for the sake of the future', as a deterrent, to prevent the offender or others who see him punished from doing wrong again (324 A–C).[16] Thus, Protagoras sees punishment not only in a legal context, but also in wider educational contexts, as in his remarks about punishment in early education (325 D).

Protagoras presents, then, these practices of Athenians and others as evidence that, at least as the Athenians believe, excellence can be imparted. Given Protagoras' epistemology, this is sufficient for him to make his point: if the Athenians so believe it, so it is for them. But note carefully: human and political excellence can be imparted, i.e. one can be made better by the agency of diverse people and institutions; but there is only teaching of it if teaching is not supposed to involve either the training in special skills or some fostering of intellectual development. Because there is no knowledge involved, neither as skills to be perfected nor as understanding to be achieved, there is also no need for special agents of education. All are teachers of virtue, and thus one might think none is (327 E).

In this, the learning of human excellence is not unlike the learning of one's mother tongue. There are no teachers of spoken Greek or English. It is true that speaking one's mother tongue is a competence that involves some skills, while this does not seem to be the case with being a good man (in the Greek or in the modern sense). But this is not the point of Protagoras' comparison. Artisans too have no teachers after they have learned their trade as apprentices, and yet they improve in their craft beyond what their master-artisans have taught them. The fact that one cannot point to specific teachers or specific learning situations in which certain skills, competences, tendencies and the like are developed does not mean these are not learned or acquired.[17]

All this, as we have seen, is in keeping with Protagoras' epistemology. As there is no objective knowledge, independent of the particular man and the particular place or time, there are no compelling reasons why one should prefer one conception of goodness over another. Rather, it is all a matter of habituation, of accustoming mind and body by doing something rather than something else. There is no giving of reasons because, for Protagoras, there are no valid reasons beyond the social norms that happen to be accepted there and then. Good, as Protagoras points out at 334 C, is a relational concept. Nothing is good *per se*, only good for something or other, or for someone or other.[18]

Protagoras' position up to this point is consistent with both egoistic hedonism and utilitarianism. The social preoccupations of the myth would seem to point to some form of social utilitarianism. But Socrates sees such utilitarianism as ultimately reducible to hedonism. Considering that Protagoras can provide no argument for qualitative differences between pleasures, the reduction of utilitarianism to hedonism seems to be implied in his myth.

True, when Socrates asks him whether he thinks knowledge is the ruling element in man, i.e. whether he thinks man is capable of acting on reasons rather than on purely psychological causes, Protagoras answers that he should be ashamed of thinking otherwise. But then, since Protagoras agrees that psychological causes (here reduced to pleasure and pain) are motives for action, he also has to provide a criterion for distinguishing those pains and pleasures which are legitimate motives for action, from an ethical point of view, from those that are not. In other words, he has to provide an independent criterion for distinguishing good psychological motives from bad ones. Should he prove incapable of doing so, any subjective psychological motive will be as good as any other, and Protagoras' claim to educate men and make them better will be found baseless.

However, Protagoras obviously cannot point to a criterion independent of the feelings of the subject himself. If for him man is the measure of all things, then he cannot escape the conclusion that there can be no motivation which is not strictly psychological. Nevertheless, Protagoras can concur with Socrates' suggestion of a 'hedonic calculus'. Here the ultimate motive is still the pursuit of pleasure and the avoidance of pain, but the absolute primacy of the immediate sensation is somewhat relented. Pleasures and pains may be weighed against one another as to their intensity, and distortions arising from the relative distances in time of the various sensations are allowed for. Yet, in themselves, regarding their moral value as motives for action, pains and pleasures are all alike.[19]

'Being overcome by pleasure' would thus be ignorance or miscalculation; one is motivated by the pleasure or the pain at hand because one does not realize that one's present action precludes in fact the attainment of a greater pleasure or the avoidance of a greater pain in the future. One possibility which Socrates does not raise here is that being overcome by pleasure is indeed ignorance or miscalculation, but ignorance or miscalculation of the proper role of pleasure in the good life. But then, in this context, he could hardly have raised such an alternative, for this would have presupposed a criterion of goodness independent of pleasure (or utility), and such a criterion Protagoras does not have.

It would seem that here Socrates has succeeded in bringing Protagoras round to his own position, that no one does wrong willfully. Rather, if one does wrong it must be in ignorance. And, accordingly, human excellence is teachable. But, again, this seemingly Socratic position is argued for from hedonistic premises. To do wrong is to act wrongly, to choose the lesser pleasure (or the greater pain) instead of the greater pleasure (or the lesser pain). There is no mention in this context of the true Socratic position, presented at the beginning of the dialogue before the interchange with Protagoras, that sees wrong action as that action which is harmful to one's soul.[20]

Protagoras is thus made to concede two vital points. On the one hand, he must acknowledge that, lacking an independent criterion of goodness, psychological motivation is the only motive for action. From this it follows that the choice of ends cannot be a matter of knowledge, but must be a question of purely subjective preferences. These preferences can be shaped and trained of course, but there would be little point in judging some preferences to be better than others.[21] Protagorean education would then be little more than social adaptation. And, notwithstanding his repeated protestations to the contrary, Protagoras would be doing no more than articulating the views of the man in the street and training people to conform to those views.[22] If social adaptation is successful, so he seems to think, then social conflict is eliminated.

On the other hand, where there may be room for some improvement on the demand for immediate gratification, such improvement turns out to depend on knowledge, i.e. on the development of reason. However, here the role of reason is purely instrumental or calculative. Reason compares pleasures and weighs them against one another. It has no interest or drive of its own. On closer examination, it turns out to be not the 'ruling element' but the 'servant'. Reason does not choose ends. It does overrule certain desires, but, when it does, it is always in favour of other desires, which are deemed upon reflection to be conducive to a greater pleasure or a lesser pain. The choice of ends is thus rational only in the sense that it involves comparison of alternatives. But the alternatives themselves are compared with each other exclusively on their hedonic values. In this sense, Protagorean justification of ends remains for Socrates (and for Plato) irrational.[23]

This knowledge which is involved in the 'hedonic calculus' is precisely the technical knowledge spurned by Protagoras earlier on in the dialogue. More specifically, it is a close relative of those mathematical sciences that were part of Hippias' fare. Socrates' calculus, however, constitutes an improvement on Hippias' mathematical art. The art of calculation is brought to bear on a vital point of Socratic ethics: conscious deliberation and justification as the distinguishing characteristics of moral action.

Yet the conception of knowledge behind the hedonic calculus is not the Socratic conception. It is not the knowledge of what is good or bad for the soul, as it is not the knowledge of what is to be sought and what is to be avoided. This difference between the Socratic and the sophistic concepts of knowledge will be examined, from a somewhat different angle, in the *Gorgias*.

Socrates' hedonic calculus is put forward in the *Protagoras* only dialectically, by way of argument. This is the best Plato can make of Protagoras' case.[24] Later, in the *Theaetetus*, Plato will show that even the notion of a hedonic calculus cannot be maintained within a strictly subjectivistic framework. Such calculus predicts that a sensation (of pain or of pleasure) will be more intense than another, when actually experienced in the future, while now, in anticipation, the reverse seems to be true. Such assertion, however, presupposes that these sensations have stable natures such as to make them susceptible to predictions of this sort. That I feel now attracted by future sensation A rather than by future sensation B (or, more exactly, that A', the anticipation of A, is now more pleasant to me than B', the anticipation of B) is a purely subjective matter. That, after having experienced A or

B or both, I do or do not reverse my judgment and come to consider *B* more pleasant to me than *A* (or vice versa), again depends only on my subjective sensations. But the prediction that I will prefer *B* to *A* (or *A* to *B*) because of certain relations that obtain (usually or necessarily) between *A* and *B*, such as relative intensities, time-distances from my point of reference in the present, etc. – this prediction must be based on grounds other than my sensations alone.[25]

The dialogue ends, as expected, on an inconclusive note. But, as in other Platonic dialogues of the same period, there are some definite lessons to be learned, if not by young Hippocrates, for the sake of whom the discussion was conducted, then by the attentive reader. Plato has ruled out social or ethical relativism as a basis for education. Protagoras' conception of adjustment to one's society as the aim of education is rejected. Further, it is a central point of Socrates' argumentation that moral and intellectual education cannot be separated. It would not do for him to accept that knowledge and reasoning play only an instrumental role in morality. Rather, moral excellence is in itself knowledge. This knowledge, however, cannot be the technical knowledge of the crafts and sciences, for this again is instrumental. Hence, the knowledge which is moral excellence is not teachable in a straightforward, ordinary-language sense.

Thus, Socrates ends up trying to prove that all moral excellences are knowledge but are not teachable, while Protagoras holds in the end that they are teachable but are not knowledge (361 A–C). This is not a particularly helpful way of expressing both positions, but Plato does that none the less, no doubt for the sake of paradox. Protagoras, however, meant that human and political excellence is, in essence, non-intellectual, but it can be nurtured, and developed by various forms of conditioning, while intellectual instruction has, by the very nature of the subject, at most a secondary role in moral and social education. Socrates, on the other hand, used the same words to maintain that human excellence is essentially intellectual or rational, although not in the sense implied by the notion of an art or a science, and therefore not teachable in that sense. What *is* the sense of reason required by his position? This was not to be stated until later, in the *Symposium* and in the *Republic*.

CHAPTER 5

The impossibility of neutrality:
Gorgias

In previous dialogues, Plato had already discussed to some extent the view that education is the teaching of, or training in, the art of success, a technique applicable indifferently to whatever aims one may entertain. The sophists claimed to be able to provide just such an education. In the earlier dialogues, however, Plato had not followed to its last consequences the contention that education can and should be neutral, that the role of the educator is to arm his students with the means to further their own ends, while the ends themselves are not of his legitimate concern. Such a position was intimated in the *Protagoras* on somewhat different grounds, but it is fully developed only in the *Gorgias*.

The problem of a neutral education – not unrelated to the interpretation of morality as a technique of living – was indeed aired by some of the sophists, particularly by Gorgias and his followers. Gorgias, as we know, denied that he taught any substantive moral doctrine.[1] He taught only rhetoric, the art of public speech, and in fact the necessary means of political activity. The *Gorgias* examines the possibility of such a theory and practice of education which is neutral towards moral questions.[2] Gorgias' view is that the teacher's business is to train his students in a technique which is desirable because conducive to personal success, but the teacher himself cannot be held responsible for the uses to which this technique is put. Plato attempts to show in this dialogue that such a 'neutral' position relies on assumptions which are not as innocent as one may suppose and, to Plato, are downright unacceptable.

Plato was convinced that form in education cannot be dissociated from content. This is the nerve of his attack on rhetoric in the *Gorgias* and in the *Phaedrus*, as well as in many passages in other dialogues.[3] The conscious choice of one manner of educational influence over another, say of uninterrupted speeches instead of dialogue, was perceived by Plato as involving fundamental commitments to certain ethical and epistemological premises rather than to certain others. In all probability, Socrates had not worked out these premises at all clearly,but he left no doubt as to where his convictions lay. It was Plato who gradually brought those presuppositions out into the open, first in the *Gorgias* and later in the *Phaedrus*. Both dialogues, and the

Gorgias in particular, can be read as essays on the relation of form and content in educational practice.

The contrast between rhetoric and dialectic is struck in the first lines of the dialogue. Gorgias, the renowned orator, is prepared to appear in a set speech. But, Socrates asks, will he also be willing to engage in a dialectical conversation? Will he be prepared to let himself too be examined, or will he insist on sticking to his rehearsed 'demonstrations'? (447 B9 ff.; cf. 448 D9–10).

The dialogue turns, this time on Socrates' initiative, on the nature of Gorgias' art itself. 'What is he?' Socrates has Chaerophon, his faithful follower, ask Gorgias. After a brief interlude between Chaerophon and Gorgias' pupil, Polus, the master himself answers.

Gorgias conceives of rhetoric, at least initially, as a purely formal technique. It is the general art of speech (449 E1). Socrates is sceptical. Each of the arts seems to have its proper object. Is rhetoric alone absolutely general? Is an art possible which is indifferent to all objects and deals equally with all? The question can be asked not only about rhetoric in a restricted sense, but also about other arts. Can there be a general method of problem-solving, which is equally applicable to all problems? Dewey for example, thought there was.[4] Or can there be a general method of instruction, which can be used irrespective of the subject-matter taught? Some of the claims of certain teaching methods of the last thirty years seem to imply that much.[5] Plato thinks otherwise. Especially, he is concerned with the moral implications of a technique which disclaims responsibility for its consequences and declares itself indifferent to moral decisions.[6]

For Plato, no technique is separated from morality. Even a 'neutral' technique, which purports not to take sides on moral questions, does assume a particular moral standpoint. Moreover, Plato maintains in the *Gorgias* as elsewhere, that knowledge cannot be misused – and therefore cannot be morally neutral.[7]

Gorgias and his followers failed to think out the relationships between rhetoric and morals, and this failure was of no little consequence. Plato saw the dangers inherent in the moral vacuum left by a neutral education; its presuppositions led on the one hand to Callicles' exaltation of power, on the other to the facile identification of the good life with material prosperity – ships, public buildings and 'standard of living'.

Far from being conducive to the good life, 'value-free' education puts a deadly weapon into the hands of the unscrupulous for the corruption of simple people who are morally only children. The alternative, providing wealth and power for the city, cannot of itself produce the good life either.[8]

Rhetoric is the art of persuasion (453 A). The emphasis is on psychological effectiveness, on the orator's ability to bring his listeners round to his point of view, irrespective of its truth or falsity, or of its moral soundness. This is only consistent with the views of the historical Gorgias on the relation between language and reality.[9] Gorgias' aim is to teach how to create an image, to control public opinion, to wield personal and political power.

Rhetoric induces subjective certainty, of course. But Plato makes clear that the subjective certainty induced by rhetoric cannot be a sign of the truth of the belief to which it is attached. Certainty or conviction can come either from having learned or from having been persuaded.[10] It is a purely psychological, not an epistemological matter. One can, therefore, have conviction about true as well as about false judgments. Learning, however, implies also an epistemological evaluation; learning that p involves not only coming to believe that p, but furthermore coming to know that p, and to say that x knows p is to imply that p is true.[11]

The objective of the political orator[12] is to influence decisions, to 'make things happen'. Political oratory is thus concerned with inducing conviction about right and wrong (474 B7 ff.). Socrates, however, thinks that such a characteristic of rhetoric is incompatible with Gorgias' former claim to the neutrality of rhetorical education. Firstly, Socrates stresses that decisions about right and wrong cannot be dissociated from knowledge of what is the case. Those who have knowledge on the matter to be decided about decide on the basis of their knowledge. It is only when knowledge is lacking or insufficient that psychological motives carry the day.[13]

Secondly, Gorgias cannot at one and the same time admit that his education has, after all, a moral content – *viz.* deliberation on matters of right and wrong – and absolve himself from possible misuses of the presumedly formal techniques he teaches his students. No one would blame the boxing instructor, says Gorgias, if people came out of the gymnasium and went around punching respectable citizens on their noses (456 C7). But the example is inadequate, says Socrates, at least on Gorgias' own premises; for, if he teaches the art of influencing deliberations on matters of right and wrong – in short, political leadership – then he must presuppose a knowledge of the substantive matters to be decided upon, or alternatively he must supply that knowledge (459 Dff.). But then rhetoric is not a mere technique of gaining influence, equally applicable to any subject. The conversation with Gorgias founders on this point.

To rhetoric Socrates opposes his dialectical method. He is careful to mark off the differences between these two ways of instruction. Dialectic proceeds step by step, by questions and answers, and at each step the questioner has to secure the respondent's assent. While rhetoric appeals to the judgment of the majority, or of the influential people ('the leaders of the public opinion'). Dialectic aims at convincing the individual alone. It is, in this sense, both anti-democratic and anti-aristocratic; the results of inquiry or of deliberation should not be influenced by show of hands, but neither should they be influenced by status, wealth, power or authority (471 Eff.). The main difference between Gorgias (and his disciples) and Socrates is in their appraisal of the role of truth in the process of decision; Socrates believes that truth has a moving power, and that by freely examining the alternatives presented to him, the respondent will – other things being equal – decide for the true alternative. For Gorgias the decision was a purely psychological matter, to which the truth-value of the alternatives was irrelevant. Rhetoric was, accordingly, the technique of efficient manipulation of the psychological conditions of persuasion.

This is not to say that Socratic and Platonic dialectics do not have a psychological aspect. Much on the contrary. In the *Phaedrus* Plato openly acknowledges the role of psychology in rhetoric.[14] But also in the earlier dialogues, one never has to do with bare opinions, but always with opinions and their inseparable emotional aspects. The Platonic dialogue is never just a match of wits over intellectual positions, but is, at the same time, a pitching of personality against personality – and the *Gorgias* is one of the best examples of the kind. Callicles is not defeated only, or even mainly, on what we would call rational grounds. What reduces him to rage and then to silence is the feeling of shame in front of his public, not the cool-headed realization of a contradiction in his premises.

Socrates' arguments at 495, as in a great many other places in this dialogue and in others, are indeed *ad hominem*. But could they be otherwise? For, psychologically speaking, why should a contradiction in one's opinions, or between one's avowed opinions and their newly disclosed implications, be of any consequence? Why not shrug it all off with a disdainful 'So what?' No doubt Plato thought that logical arguments should be psychologically compelling. On the other hand, he knew full well that people – most people – fail to be convinced by such arguments. The very fact that one comes to be bothered by a contradiction is a significant psychological (and educational) achievement. At some minimal level perhaps all of us are stirred (or at least tickled) by contradictions.[15] But Plato apparently thought that, in most if not in all cases, this minimum is not sufficient, by itself, to change our deep-seated psychic laziness; the ascent from the cave in the *Republic* is violently and painfully enforced against the subject's will.[16] Thus, the elenchus implies not only disentangling logical howlers and dispelling ambiguities, but also clarifying the accompanying obscure and half-conscious emotions that divert the eye from truth and coarsen one's feeling for the unnaturalness of illogicality.

It is well known that the logical analysis of the Socratic elenchus and of the Platonic dialogue does not take us very far. Alone, it does not explain, for example, why Meno misses the double play on 'learning' at 87 B–C and 89 C, or why Callicles quits the field at 505 C. In fact, it does not explain why the *Gorgias*, like many other early dialogues, ends in a complete breakdown of communication.

The Platonic dialogue is true philosophical drama. It is not the presentation of an argument that stands on its own feet; it is the story of the interaction of two souls in all their modes of expression. The intellectual level is one of them; another is the emotional level, where the clash between the personalities occurs. Any attempt to understand the movement of the dialogue solely in logical terms is bound to be misleading, just as no concrete learning process can be understood in purely cognitive terms.

Logical fallacies have thus a definite function in the dialogue. Their role is not only logical, such as emphasizing ambiguities and hidden assumptions, but often they aim also at leading the opponent astray, so as to have him committed as deeply as possible to his (mistaken) position, for only thus can he come to feel his ignorance when his position is finally disproved. Socrates' cat-and-mouse game with the boy in the geometry lesson in the *Meno* is a case in point. Before allowing the boy to consider the right answer, Socrates makes him try in full all the alternatives he can think of himself. Only after the boy has exhausted his possibilities and, seeing no way out, cries in despair, 'By Zeus, Socrates, I don't know!', only then is Socrates prepared to bail him out. Conversely, lack of commitment to one's answers pre-empts any possibility of fruitful inquiry. At a certain point in the *Gorgias*, for example, Callicles abdicates his commitment to the success of the conversation, and continues to answer only 'for consistency's sake'. There the real dialogue with Socrates ends. And a few pages further, Socrates can even forgo Callicles' participation in the conversation and himself play both roles of questioner and answerer (494 Aff.).[17]

The logical steps of the argument are the surface structure of the dialogue. The real educational drama is given in what happens besides, or in spite of, the logical structure. For Plato, when intellectual activity is conceived of as a mere manipulation aiming only at consistency, it has no real worth. But this is precisely Callicles' view of reason, and the view of Gorgias, his teacher. Reason is for them purely instrumental, with no intrinsic aims. Plato thought this separation of reason – that which deliberates about means – from whatever it is that chooses ends to be not only false but also immoral. The conception of reason as formal, manipulative, neutral, leads to a theory of instruction and learning concerned with *techne*, with know-how which is dissociated from ends, in so far as it is applicable to all ends indifferently. On this view, the role of the teacher or instructor is to teach or to instruct, namely to supply the learner with the information and the skills required for whatever he (the learner) would want to do. What the learner may want to do is none of the teacher's business, either because the teacher cannot know it or because he is not allowed to interfere with it. The portrait of Callicles in the *Gorgias* is a study in the ultimate development of such a conception.

Plato's reaction to Gorgias' idea of a neutral education comes out loud and clear. The historical Gorgias himself had compared the effect of rhetoric on the soul to the effect of medicine on the body.[18] Plato turns the tables on him. Medicine is a corrective art, based on the knowledge of the proper state of the body, to which it has to be restored. Its spiritual equivalent is the art of the judge. Education – or, as Plato has it, statesmanship or legislation – is the regulative or normative art which creates in the soul that desirable state in the first place. The kind of education Gorgias procures is not based on knowledge of what is desirable for the soul, but on the substitution of the actually desired for the desirable. As cosmetics and tailoring try to achieve a spurious beauty instead of the real beauty that can only be got by nature and exercise, and as cooking aims at producing a feeling of pleasure which may be medically unsound – so too, concludes Plato, forensic rhetoric seems to correct the soul, and the sophistic method appears to educate it, but both are based on the agreeable and the desired, not on the desirable (463 E5–466 A3). Such an education as offered by Gorgias offers quick, insubstantial gratification to the uneducated. At best, it is disappointing and frustrating, for it cannot deliver what it promises. Like cooking and cosmetics, it panders to public taste instead of trying to change it. At worst, it takes advantage of the gullibility and weakness of the many for the advantage of the few.

Gorgias has an honourable conception of his profession.[19] But Polus, his pupil, is quick to grasp that, on Gorgias' premises, a case can be made with relative ease for an art of leadership which concerns itself only with effectiveness, without regard for the uses to which it is put. Once political leadership is defined as the art of 'making things happen through others',[20] then there is no intrinsic reason why its efficiency should be restricted by moral considerations, except perhaps as a concession to social conventions. Polus, however, thinks such concessions a result of shame, which he interprets, like Callicles, as a symptom of the lack of courage to stick to the consequences of one's opinions. If only one were strong enough to withstand social pressure, one would not submit to suffering evil when one could do evil with impunity instead. What is morally approved of and what is naturally desirable are two incompatible things and no one would go against his nature if he had the power and the courage to further his own interests and disregard social reproach (467f.).[21]

Socrates' main argument against Polus is short (474 C4–476 A2).[22] Socrates suggests, and Polus agrees, that things are called noble or fine (*kala*) on account of their utility or the pleasure they promote or both. This distinction is not unlike that between extrinsic and intrinsic values, elaborated on by Socrates elsewhere in the dialogue (cf. 467 Cff.). Now Socrates presents Polus with the following disjunctive syllogism.

If *A* is more reproachable than *B*, then:

(1) *A* is more painful than *B*; or
(2) *A* is worse (i.e. more harmful) than *B*; or
(3) both.

Therefore, if doing evil is more reproachable than suffering evil, then:

(1) it is more painful; or
(2) it is worse (=more harmful); or
(3) both.

But
    doing evil (1) is not more painful,
    therefore also not (3) both,
    therefore (2) it is more harmful (=worse).

Thus, doing evil is not only morally disapproved of (reproachable), but also naturally undesirable. But, of course, Socrates does not yet specify the nature of the harm inflicted by the doing of evil. He is speaking the current utilitarian language, but he is stretching it beyond its limits, and will eventually try to express in it a non-utilitarian position.

It was Polus who identified goodness with utility (475 A3).[23] The substitution does not formally affect the argument,[24] and Socrates needs it in any case. Polus is defeated on his own terms, since he was forced to go back on his assertion that what is noble is different from what is good, which he understands as that which has utility value. Socrates, on the other hand, is equivocating, for the goodness he has in mind, if it is utility at all, is not the kind of utility Polus described in his eulogy of the tyrannical life.[25]

Callicles disagrees with Polus in that Callicles denies the separation between the good, understood as the useful, and the right, or the morally approved of. But Callicles interprets the right as the good;

morality is nothing but the self-fulfilment of the individual. However, Callicles takes a strictly individualistic view of self-fulfilment. Society is nothing but the battleground of personalities. For him, as for Thrasymachus in *Republic* I, the self-fulfilment of one individual is bound to conflict with the self-fulfilment of another individual, since desire as they understand it has no instrinsic limits. Thus, the various individual drives toward fulfilment necessarily become entangled in a struggle for domination.

Such a view could be taken to support a blanket endorsement of whatever is the outcome of the struggle for supremacy. A man's right or a group's right would then be equated with their actual success in imposing their will and having their way. This is in fact Thrasymachus' position; there is no measure to a ruler's legitimacy other than the actual fact of his rule. This is a naturalistic position, which must give up any evaluation of the use of power and restrict itself to registering that power has been wielded successfully. On this view, as Socrates points out, the rule of the many and the rule of the few would be on a par, and in neither case would there be any legitimation beyond the actual fact.

Callicles makes clear that this is *not* his view (489 Bff.). The mere fact cannot be the justification for someone's or some group's ruling. Rather, there are those who are naturally fitter to rule, although they may not in fact rule. Callicles, unlike Thrasymachus, is not an amoralist. On the contrary, he too upholds a morality of nature, albeit one opposed to Socrates'. Nevertheless, in some points, Callicles' morality is dangerously close to Socrates' (or to Plato's). Is not Plato's contention in the *Republic* that the best should rule by right? Moreover, does not Plato acknowledge Callicles' point that the ruler by nature, the true ruler, would put himself above the law? The crucial difference is in the purpose of the rule of the best. For Callicles, nature's law is that the best should rule and increase his lot. The ruler rules for his own benefit. Whereas for Plato the ruler rules for the objective benefit of the state and not for himself (483 D).[26]

The happy and successful man is, in Callicles' view, the free man. Callicles' conception of freedom is a privative one; to be free is not to be subject to restrictions, whether imposed by others or by oneself (491 E5–6). Thus, the happy and successful man, being free, is he whose will is not hemmed in by restrictions of any kind. But this is not enough; he must have the intelligence to devise the implementation of his desires, be they great as they might, and the courage to carry through his plans without shirking before accepted opinion or ingrained custom. Reason, for Callicles, has no end of its own, just as Gorgias' rhetoric had none; it is a neutral instrument for the implementation of extraneous ends. Man's desires, in Callicles' view, and foremost the will to power, are not rational. For Plato, all that is rational has a limit and can be explained, whereas desire, on this view, is essentially inexplicable and irrational, and has no justification beyond its very demand for gratification. This is a sort of psychological naturalism. The great man is he who does not restrain his psychic sources but lets them flow unchecked. The 'inferior' men are those who deny their own nature by confining it within the limits of conventional morality, or else those whose inner psychic sources are, from the beginning, poor enough not to conflict with accepted values.

Callicles sees the essence of man in his ever-increasing will. A man who does not will is a dead man. Callicles would have said with Hobbes that 'Felicity is a continual progress of the desire, from one object to another; the attaining of the former, being still but the way to the latter.'[27] Such a will has no set characteristics, no determined nature. Therefore it is, in principle, unbound as to its intensity and its possible objects; all objects are equally possible objects of the will, and their worth comes to them from the intensity with which they are willed. But this intensity cannot be imposed on the will. On the contrary, the act of desiring is primary. Nothing prevents anything from being willed, and reason only helps in attaining the objects willed. Callicles draws the conclusions from Gorgias' position; the technique is neutral concerning the possible ends of the will, and all objects of desire are of equal worth.

On his view, then, excellence cannot be taught, since necessary conditions of it are a great will, courage and intelligence. Indeed, the rhetorician does not teach excellence, but only puts into the student's hands an instrument for the fulfilment of his desires and his will to power.

For Callicles, then, there is no education of the will in the sense of a redirection of the will towards appropriate objects. Because no object is more appropriate than any other, the role of education is restricted to the strengthening of the will and to the preparation of the intellect to serve it. It is, in fact, the education of a strong character.

Callicles presupposes a hedonistic basis for morality, or at least a view according to which the good is the utility for the individual as determined by the individual himself. On this view, the individual's concept of good is incorrigible. It is true that this conception of the individual is only of what is good for him, but – on Callicles' view – the individual is entitled to try to implement this good even if it conflicts with other individuals' goods as conceived by them.

Socrates denies the hedonistic premise. The good is not identical with pleasure or with subjective utility. For one thing, he says, pleasure and pain can co-exist in respect of the same thing (469 Eff.);[28] good and evil cannot. More importantly, Socrates holds that an individual's utility is objectively determinable, and therefore one could be wrong about what one 'really' wants. Education, for

Socrates, must therefore include also education for willing appropriate objects. Power in itself cannot be a good, as Socrates implies in the example of the madman with a knife (469 C–470 C). Power is good or bad only in connexion with the ends which it serves and the ways in which it is used.

For Polus, as for Hume, the choice of ends is not an intellectual matter; desire alone has ends, and reason only provides the means of implementing these ends.[29] But if so, Plato seems to think, there can be no other criterion for the evaluation of ends, except the degree to which they are desired. This can hardly be the case, Plato argues. Obviously, some things are desired not for their own sake but for the sake of other things. Those which are desired only for the sake of something else have thus no proper, or intrinsic, value, but their value or desirability is due to that to which they are instrumental. Plato's conclusion in the exchange with Polus is that there must be things which have intrinsic value and for their sake we do whatever we do.

But this means in fact that the appreciation of the value of any action or thing (if it is not intrinsic – a point Plato does not make[30]) is dependent on the appreciation of its connexions to other actions or things. In so far, it is not subjective, but objective. It is not a matter of choosing whatever one fancies, but of using one's reason in appraising the real benefits beyond the satisfaction of the moment (466 E).[31] Men may desire things and in so far as they desire them these things seem to them good. However, so Socrates' argument goes, one could possibly will a thing under a misapprehension of its instrumental or intrinsic goodness. It is true that men desire the good (or good things), but one could be mistaken in one's understanding of what the good consists of. One could, therefore, desire things which are in fact bad, provided one were under the misapprehension that those things are good. But then one wants these only under a false description and as a result of such a false description (here included the false description of an instrumental good as final). This makes possible the distinction between what a man wants and what he 'really' wants, or between the object of a person's desires and his real good. As has been pointed out more than once, this is a dangerous distinction, in that it can and did allow disregard for people's genuine wishes in the name of their 'real' good.[32] On the other hand, it is a mainstay of Plato's philosophy that education implies the directing of one's desires toward appropriate objects.[33]

For Socrates, this re-directing of the desires is intimately tied up with the attainment of knowledge. He who has learned carpentry is a carpenter, and he who has learned music or medicine is a musician or a doctor. Similarly, he concludes, 'he who had learned the just things is just'. No doubt, Socrates is referring to his principle that to know the good is to do it. Socrates pressed hard the parallel of morality and the arts. But the knowledge he had in mind, that knowledge which made his possessor just or good, could not be a set of rules, such as those of the craftsman. Rather, as Plato develops it in later dialogues, it is the knowledge of one's true interest, which can be based only on the wider knowledge of man's place in the world (460 A–C).[34]

The full answer is given by Plato only in the *Republic*, and also in the *Symposium* and the *Phaedrus*. However, the last part of the *Gorgias* already gives us some anticipation of it, without much of the metaphysical apparatus that Plato was to develop later.

The good, so it is agreed between Socrates and Callicles, is the end or the aim of all making and doing, even in the minimal sense of being that for the sake of which one does whatever is done. But the end or aim of an action is a principle of order, in that it determines the sequence and appropriateness of the steps to be taken. I do A, and then B, and then C, because C is conducive to Z, which I want to achieve, and B is conducive to C, and A to B. The action, considered as a whole, is seen as composed of a series of steps as parts of that whole. The parts and their sequence cannot be arbitrary, but are of necessity determined by the end envisaged. Thus, the end restricts the parts in relation to each other and in relation to the whole, since none of the parts (or single steps) stands on its own right but each is determined by its relation to the other parts (e.g., B's being conducive to C) and to the whole (i.e. being part of the organized series which produces Z). The excellence of anything is its perfection, i.e. its ability to perform its function or attain its end in the best way. Thus, if the end is a principle of order, that thing will best be able to perform its function if it incorporates such order as is implied by its end or function.

The questionable step will be, of course, the application of this reasoning to persons, both as having themselves a function and as having their excellence adequately defined by the function they perform in society. In this, our concept of a person obviously differs from Plato's, if indeed he had such a concept.

Plato draws some interesting conclusions from his analysis. First, even on a *prima facie* instrumental approach, reason is not indifferent to questions of good and evil, and of human excellence. On the contrary, the teleological aspect of reason is in fact constitutive of the distinction between good and evil. Secondly, one could be mistaken as to the goodness or badness of one's several actions since one could be mistaken as to the relations of one's actions to each other within the framework of one's integrated life. Thirdly, Callicles' view of excellence as the ability to satisfy one's unlimited desires is countered by the conclusion that excellence (*arete*) and success (*eudaimonia*) necessarily imply the mutual limitation of means and ends. This applies not only to the individual alone but also to the individual within the society. The law is thus not arbitrary, but has a basis in the teleological nature of human action and of the world itself. This, however, is not argued here, only stated in a rather dogmatic manner.

Callicles could still answer that he can maintain a self-seeking morality without falling prey to desires working at cross-purposes. He could still use his reason to lead a coherent and efficient but utterly egoistic and exploitative life. His personality would not be any the less coherent for that. One need not be a madman to be a successful tyrant; one need only get one's priorities straight.

But Callicles' main point seems to be throughout that the use of reason is confined to the implementation of one's desires against outside opposition. Thus, one should have the courage not to balk before the accepted conceptions of right and wrong, and one should be resourceful enough to confront adverse circumstances and outwit one's opponents. Callicles does not consider, however, the possibility of inner conflicts, i.e. the possibility of conflicting or mutually exclusive drives in the same person.

Plato's answer to Callicles is twofold. As an observation on human nature, Plato does not believe that anyone could be shameless enough to disregard completely the accepted values of society. When Callicles sticks to his view that evaluation is a purely subjective matter, and no pleasure is better than any other except in that it is actually desired at a given moment, Socrates presses him to accept – on his own premises – that the pleasures of male prostitution are as good as any other, for those who enjoy them. Callicles is shaken: 'Are you not ashamed, Socrates, to bring the discussion to such matters?' (494 E). But he is prepared to agree, for the sake of the argument and not to lose face. For Callicles, shame is a symptom of failure of nerve or of lack of courage; for Socrates, it is a residue of reason on the level of common sense.

The second part of Plato's answer consists in pointing out that 'to get one's priorities straight' is precisely to recognize that one cannot let one's desires flow freely, as they could interfere with each other, since it may be impossible to gratify them all. Internal conflicts are a fact of psychological life, and one's happiness and success depend primarily on the resolution of one's internal conflicts.

Polus' man with a knife is a fool and a madman, even if he has sufficient power to escape punishment, for he necessarily is unable to organize his drives within one coherent personality. His soul is diseased in the same way that one's body is diseased when its unhealthy appetites get the better of it, causing imbalance and eventual disintegration. To escape punishment of the diseased soul is like refusing to submit the sick body to the doctor's treatment, fearing the lesser evil instead of the greater (479ff.).[35]

There is more to the concept of mental health in the *Gorgias* than mere allegory.[36] Plato does not introduce the analogy of the doctor and the judge only as a rhetorical device. The contention that desires should not be satisfied without limits is backed by several analyses of the teleology of actions and the relations of means and ends. This teleology, Plato asserts, is present also in man and indeed in the whole cosmos (503 D–504 A, cf. 508 A). But he does not set out to argue this in the *Gorgias*. Thus, while Plato may not yet have had a full theory to support his new concept of mental health, he did from the beginning see it as an integral part of his philosophy.

CHAPTER 6

Sophistic or Socratic?
Euthydemus

The *Euthydemus* is a caricature, to be sure, but, as with all good caricature, it has a serious intent. It shows the degeneration of the sophistic approach to education, in some of its aspects. More importantly, at the same time, it sets apart the methods and effects of Socratic education from those of its sophistic counterpart.

Euthydemus and Dionysodorus, the two sophist brothers, are reminiscent of the great sophists of the *Protagoras* in more than one way. They are polymaths like Hippias, and at one time or another have taught a variety of arts, from forensic oratory to armoured combat. Also, they have Prodicus' penchant for linguistic analysis. But, most of all, they are Protagoras' epigones, down to the smallest details: they walk around the courtyard with their entourage of disciples, who follow them from city to city; they promise to teach human excellence with speed and efficiency; with the change of fashions, they have come to think of the other sciences (apart from the teaching of excellence) as valueless; they deny the possibility of contradiction; they can argue equally well either side of a case.[1] But whereas Protagoras had intellectual stature and moral integrity, the two brothers are no more than unscrupulous quacks. Nevertheless, Euthydemus and Dionysodorus are a direct and presumably inevitable consequence of Protagoras' views, much as Callicles is a consequence of Gorgias'.

For the two brothers, philosophy has become the science of argumentation. They are experts of verbal fight, capable of refuting any position, true or false. It is not irrelevant that the brothers had previously taught the *pancration*; in this Greek variety of 'catch-as-catch-can' there were few restrictions on what was permitted, whether the opponent was standing or had already been downed. The brothers' type of argumentation is not much different. As in the other types of litigation they practised, such as forensic oratory and armoured combat, victory over the opponent is the only goal, and means are evaluated solely by their efficacy in achieving that goal. The brothers too, like Socrates, equate virtue with knowledge. But their concept of virtue is that of the knowledge how to succeed at all costs, how to get the better of others in any circumstance. Hence they teach mockeries of the traditional excellences: litigation instead of justice; techniques

43

of fighting instead of courage; and, above all, eristic instead of wisdom.

The brothers' logic is purely formal and argumentative, equally appropriate to any content or circumstance. Since the technique of argumentation is presumed indifferent to the content of the argument, refuting the truth is, for the two sophists, a live possibility. There is a technique of refutation that works equally well on either side of the case. Not so for Socrates: 'If I am not mistaken,' he says to Dionysodorus, 'even you will not refute me, clever as you are' (287 E4–5). Socratic elenchus is the refutation of false or confused ideas. But truth cannot be refuted. There are two sides to each argument only so long as we do not know on which side the truth lies. Socrates, indeed, claimed not to know. He kept therefore both sides of the argument as possibilities. But this did not exclude that one side was right and the other wrong.

Protagoras claimed to be able to teach excellence and to make his students better 'from day to day'. Socrates, no less than Isocrates, doubts the claims of that 'new-found art of making good men out of bad' (285 B4–5).[2] For him, education is too complex a matter to be summarized in a collection of fool-proof techniques. But the two sophists promise even more; they are capable of 'delivering' or 'handing down' excellence 'in the quickest way' (273 D8–9). Indeed, as Socrates remarks at 272 B10, 'last year or the year before they were not yet wise'. Plato is drawing an exaggerated picture, but the point is valid; there are no shortcuts in education, no crash-courses in virtue. Instant wisdom is a sham; the way of education is long and difficult (somewhat like the curriculum of the *Republic*, he thought), and, what is worse, its results are uncertain until one reaches the very end of it –if one ever does. It is true that Socrates seems to achieve now and then some encouraging results with his method of interrogation, but he never claims that, e.g., Clinias in the *Euthydemus* or the unnamed boy in the *Meno* have actually attained wisdom or knowledge. He only prepared Clinias for learning, aroused his interest. It would be a good thing if excellence and wisdom could be handed down (274 A).[3] But these are not the sort of things that can be transmitted; they can only be slowly developed by each person for himself, with some outside help and no guarantee of success.

The first question raised by Socrates, as soon as the conversation with the sophists gets going, is the question of motivation. Has the student to be willing to learn, or convinced that he can or should learn from his teacher, or is this unnecessary (274 D7)? If teaching and education consist chiefly in the handing down of certain beliefs, then the student's involvement is minimal. It is somewhat like one's involvement in receiving an object which is being given; there need not be much, if any, activity or initiative on the part of the receiver. In the case of intellectual content, one could, at most, imagine the necessity of suitable preparation, as in Herbart's once influential model of the apperceptive mass.[4] But, in this case, in so far as the interest has to be aroused, it is in order to supersede emotional or intellectual elements which may block the way to new information; it is not in order to bring the student to seek or produce knowledge himself.

Therefore there need not be any personal relation whatsoever between teacher and student. When asked if the brothers would mind conversing with Clinias, Euthydemus answers that it does not matter to them, so long as the boy is willing to answer their questions. They merely need a respondent (275 B–C).[5] They are not worried, as Socrates is, by the possibility that the boy's studies may do him harm rather than good (275 A–B).[6] For them, all respondents are equal. And, to a certain extent, they too are interchangeable; it does not matter too much who leads the questioning, the one or the other, so long as it abides by the rules of the art (cf. 297 A). Socrates, on the other hand, at least as Plato depicts him later, would sometimes refuse to renew his association with followers who left him. He felt that some persons would not profit from him, on grounds of intelligence or personality. A personal relationship between teacher and student (if the relationship between Socrates and his friends can be so described) was for him a necessary condition of education.[7]

Once the sophistic display has actually started, Socrates' first words stress his interpretation of the elenctic process as distinct from eristic. At 275 D, Euthydemus asks young Clinias a question not unlike Meno's: 'Who are those who learn, the wise or the ignorant?'[8] As Clinias seems perplexed by the question, Socrates entreats him to answer 'courageously, whichever answer it seems to you. For,' he says, 'maybe you are to get the greatest of benefits.' Socrates ironically presents the two brothers' sophistry as on a par with his own elenchus. Each question requires a courageous answer, no matter which, so long as it is what really seems to the answerer to be the case. But Dionysodorus immediately makes clear that Clinias' answers do not matter in the least. Whatever the boy says, the outcome will be the same: 'And I foretell you, Socrates, that whichever way he answers, the boy will be refuted.' The technique is so set up that the interaction of teacher and student plays no significant role in it. There is only a sequence of steps to be followed, and this technique can be mastered with relative ease. It is, in effect, a teacher-proof and student-proof method. In the sophistic elenchus, the cards are stacked and there is no way in which the answerer can alter the course of the argument.

Despite its superficial similarity to the sophistic interrogation, Socratic elenchus differs from it in one crucial aspect, which is not immediately apparent in the written dialogue. In the Socratic dialogue each of Socrates' questions brings the answerer to a road fork, so that at each point in the development of the conversation it is the answerer himself who must decide which way to take, according to his own convictions. The course of the dialogue is jointly determined by Socrates' presentation, and his partner's choice, of alternatives. Socrates' emphasis on the joint search for an answer is not mere rhetoric. He leads the search, but it is his partner who confirms or denies the suggestions made by Socrates. When this is done in good faith – and it is not always so – then both sides are responsible for the outcome of the dialogue. Because the dialogue is always carried out within a context, not all possible alternatives are explored in one dialogue. Frequently only one proposed solution or one type of proposed solutions is examined. Alternatives that were not followed up in one dialogue are sometimes developed by Plato in another, sometimes dropped altogether. Taken as a whole, the schema of all possible bifurcations provides a sort of matrix of possibilities to be explored. Rarely is such a schema to be found in one single dialogue.[9]

It follows that instruction in earnest is conceived by Socrates as essentially an individual matter. It depends on the personal convictions of the learner at each stage of the discussion, and for different people the discussion branches off differently at different points. No two processes of instruction can be alike, not only in their psychological aspects, regarding how instruction is conducted, but also in their content, in what is actually learned or discovered.

Socrates correctly sees the two sophists' equivocations on words as degenerate descendents of Prodicus' insistence on the correctness of names (277 E). But he considers such linguistic distinctions mere play. They do not teach us anything about the world itself. Such knowledge allows us to make fun of others in a rather broad way, but little else.

Eventually, the brothers' too simplistic approach to language is bound to break down. Their view of language is none too subtle: the function of language is to designate; therefore, to speak truly is to succeed in designating, to speak falsely to fail. But if one speaks, one obviously succeeds in doing something, namely speaking, which is supposed to be just a way of designating, like pointing. Obviously, if one points, one has succeeded in pointing. Therefore, if one speaks, one necessarily speaks truly. Ctesippus spots the flaw in the argument. 'Speaking of' is not a two-place predicate, like 'pointing at', but a three-place predicate, like 'naming' or 'identifying'. Not 'A speaks of x', but 'A speaks of x as N' (cf. 'A points at x', and 'A names x "N"', or 'A identifies x as N'). To speak falsely of x is then not to fail to speak of x, but to speak of x as M (when x is in fact N). To call a spade a spade is to speak truly. To speak falsely is to call it something else; it is not to fail to speak (284 C7–8).[10]

But Dionysodorus and Euthydemus will have none of this inter-pretation. They stick to their view of 'speaking of' as a two-place predicate, and accordingly allow modifiers such as 'truly' and 'falsely' to be understood only adverbally, i.e. as referring to the act of speak-ing or designating. Thus, speaking truly is speaking in a certain man-ner, comparable to speaking slowly or loudly. Further, if to speak truly is to speak of what is as it is, then, on their view, this amounts to speaking of each thing in a manner appropriate to it, as speaking badly of bad men, and tastelessly of tasteless men (284 C9).[11]

This position is consistent, as far as it goes, but it flies in the face of the facts. The sophist brothers' argument is self-defeating, as Socrates points out; if there is no contradiction, or, alternatively, if one cannot speak falsely, then refutation too is impossible (286 E2ff.).[12] But Plato does not seem to think that there is a formal contradiction in the argument, only a pragmatic one. When Socrates points out to Dionysodorus that on his own view refutation is impossible, Euthydemus takes over. Since the contradiction is between the prop-osition 'Refutation is impossible' and *Dionysodorus'* demand that Socrates refute him, a change of speakers should take care of the problem. If contradiction is impossible, so are error and teaching. This is, of course, Protagoras' view, only Protagoras is much subtler.

Pragmatic contradiction can be dismissed if one is stubbornly pre-pared to disregard the need for consistency between one's several utterances or between one's utterances and one's actions. The price is too high, but this is precisely what Dionysodorus does. He sees him-self at liberty to disown what he had said before. Each argument is considered in isolation from the others. There is no overall coherence (or even consistency) in his argumentation and no commitment to the positions taken (287 A5ff.).[13]

Socrates too changes his views in the course of many a dialogue, at least apparently (e.g. in the *Protagoras* or in the *Meno*), and he cer-tainly has his respondents change their minds. But he always stresses the consistency of the whole argumentation and the commitment to finding out what the case is. When one changes one's views, it should be done in honesty and responsibility for one's utterances, for the sake of a greater overall consistency, not because of expediency in argumentation for its own sake.

Because Dionysodorus' approach is purely linguistic and formal, with no regard for either the coherence of the argument or for the matter discussed itself, the conversation degenerates into personal insult. If one is not committed to one's answer and conducts the inquiry on a purely verbal level, without paying attention to things as they are, then there is nothing one could not say, ridiculous or shame-ful or absurd. Eventually, once semantics have been discarded as not formal enough, even the rules of syntax are not of much help. Language itself breaks down (303 A7–8).

The consequences of such an education are obvious. What can be picked up quickly is only such a spurious art of argumentation. Its results can be seen in the exchange of insults earlier in the dialogue, between Ctesippus and Euthydemus (289 Bff.). Ctesippus makes progress indeed in the argumentative art and manages in a short time to master it well enough to engage the sophists in their own game. However, his youthful impetuousness prevents him from reaching Clinias' stage. Ctesippus can see through the sophists' tricks but, because of his psychical make-up, he is not able to participate in the serious discussion.

On the other hand, Socrates himself gives an example of the type of conversation which will motivate a mind to the pursuit of wisdom (278 Eff.). He starts, as usual, with the obvious and close at hand. All men desire happiness. This happiness is preliminarily described in conventional terms: first as the possession of the goods of the body, such as health and beauty; further as having good birth, power and honour; and lastly as possessing such virtues as temperance, justice and courage. But on further examination it is found that only wisdom brings success, and therefore all the so-called goods are in fact indifferent as to goodness or badness.[14] If accompanied by wisdom they are good and bring happiness; if not, they are liable to be misused. This was an example of the protreptic argument Socrates had asked for at 275 A. Clinias is now at least initially motivated to philosophize, i.e. to seek wisdom, in so far as he thinks it is to his advantage to do so. The question whether wisdom is teachable is passed over (282 C), since it would require a full investigation of its nature and of its relation to happiness – to which a great part of the *Republic* is devoted.

Even without going into such a long inquiry, a second, more limited question is in order: Is wisdom the whole of knowledge or is it a specific knowledge? In other words, is there such a science of happiness and excellence, or is the aim of education encyclopedic knowledge? The *Republic* will claim that these are not alternatives; wisdom, as the knowledge of the right conduct of one's affairs and of the affairs of the state, is in fact synoptical (but not encyclopedic) knowledge. The difference between encyclopedic and synoptical knowledge will be made clear only in the *Republic* and in the *Phaedrus*.[15]

Now philosophy, Socrates summarizes, is the acquisition (or possession)[16] of knowledge. How this acquisition comes about, or what such a possession consists of, is left unexplained. It is implied that it is not a handing over of information, and that it is, in effect, the process Clinias is undergoing even in that moment. Some analytical discussion of such a process – one of the very few educational successes in Plato's dialogues[17] – is undertaken in the *Meno*.

Here Plato is interested in the nature of that knowledge which constitutes wisdom, i.e. of that knowledge which was agreed upon to be worthwhile. Socrates picks up the utilitarian line he has been following and suggests that the knowledge worth acquiring is that which will benefit us. So far, this is nothing but an explication of the utilitarian assumptions of the argument. But, as already agreed, nothing is beneficial if not wisely used. Thus, the knowledge worth acquiring must be the knowledge of using things, not of making them or getting them.[18]

The need for a hierarchy of crafts and sciences is thus argued for. Such a hierarchy is the base of the difference between encyclopedic knowledge, furthered by the sophists, and synoptical knowledge favoured by Plato. The organizing knowledge is the art of kingship, identified with politics. Individual education thus becomes inextricably linked with political thinking. There is here a prefiguration of the *Republic*; not only the philosopher-king is presented as the final outcome of education, and himself an educator, but also the hierarchical relations are hinted at between the sciences, dialectic and the political art.[19]

However, the art of the philosopher-king, when seen as the art of educating men, presents some difficulties. For one, it does not seem to have, as the other arts, a product of its own. In a sense, one could say that the role of the ruler as educator is to give the citizens a share of knowledge.[20] His art consists in having the state infused with knowledge, though in different degrees, according to the capacity of each. The art of kingship is thus the art of making others good. There can be for Plato no separation between politics and education, or ideologically neutral education.

In what way does the art of kingship make us good? In what way is it different from the 'newly discovered art of making good men out of bad'? If in this way we are capable of educating others, and these still others, etc., then we have done nothing to find what this art is. A characterization of education in terms of 'initiation' or preservation and continuation of the patterns of the society or of culture will not do without further specificaiton. Plato is after the content of such an art.[21]

But apparently the analogy to the other arts, which led us to look for the content, is misleading. The contents of the art of kingship cannot be universal – 'carpentry, and cobbling, and all the rest' – and it cannot be the knowledge of itself.[22] These questions cannot be adequately discussed in the context of this dialogue and they are merely hinted at as a demonstration of the Socratic method.

Socrates' inquiries in the *Euthydemus* reach an impasse and seem to lead nowhere. Similarly, the sophists' tricks too lead nowhere. Yet, these negative conclusions are of different types. Socrates' *aporia* is a sign that further investigation is needed, and is intended to incite the partner to such investigation. The sophistic quandary puts down its victim and makes him despair from inquiry.

But many felt this was what Socrates too was doing; putting down people, leading them in circles by means of sophistic tricks and finally paralysing them with his questions from which there was no escape. The *Euthydemus* sets out the difference between the Socratic and the sophistic methods. But Plato is well aware that the difference is not easy to grasp. At the end of the dialogue, back to the frame-story, Crito relates an outsider's view of Socrates; Socrates seemed to him ridiculous and embarrassing. Crito himself – no fool, seriously concerned with the education of his sons, and Socrates' friend – agrees, to some extent, with this appraisal of Socrates (305 Af.; cf. 307 A1–2).[23]

It takes a keen eye – the eye of Plato, presumably – to spot the difference and to be aware of the problems inherent in the Socratic method. It can often be misused or mistaken for ridicule. This happened to Socrates more than once.[24] An educational approach which uses irony is bound to be limited to the few. For Plato, the political man, the difficulties would be obvious. But Plato could also appreciate the positive value of Socrates' irony when properly understood.

CHAPTER 7

The concept of learning: *Meno*

'Can you tell me, Socrates. . . ?'

Meno's very first words summarize his conception of learning; he wants to be told. Learning is for him a passive reception of information. As against Socrates' repeated entreatings – 'Tell me yourself, Meno' (71 D1), 'By the gods, Meno, what do you yourself say excellence is' (71 D4–5) – Meno can only ask again and again, 'No, but you tell me, Socrates' (75 B1), 'But I ask you, Socrates, so that you tell me' (75 A10–13).

Uncharacteristically for a Platonic dialogue, the *Meno* has no setting and no frame story. Meno's question has no apparent context (as, e.g., the *Euthyphro*), it does not arise from any situation demanding an answer (as the *Laches*), it does not develop out of a preliminary conversation (as the *Lysis* or the *Republic*). Whatever preceded Meno's question is irrelevant to it. Meno expects the answer to be given without any regard to what has come before; he expects it to be given unambiguously in the terms of the question alone.

The *Meno* is, among other things, an inquiry into the concept of learning. The first part of the dialogue consists of Meno's attempts at defining human excellence (*arete*). Except for some peculiarities – the rather broad subject, the abrupt opening, etc. – it reads like one of the smaller Socratic dialogues, such as the *Laches* or the *Euthyphro*. As expected in a Socratic dialogue, Meno's three attempts at definition fail. But then the dialogue takes an unexpected turn. Meno rebels against Socrates' procedures, complaining that, far from helping his interlocutors, Socrates paralyses them: 'And which way will you look, Socrates, for that which you do not know at all what it is? What sort of thing among those you don't know will you aim at in your search? Or even if you hit upon it, how will you know that this is what you did not know?' (80 D5–8).

Meno's accusation is serious; it calls into question the foundations of the Socratic method itself. No wonder Socrates' conversations all end up in *aporia*, in bewilderment, and Socrates never gets anywhere. Socrates' method is such that it necessarily closes off all possibility of inquiry.

Socrates himself, no less than Meno, sees inquiry as essentially a matter of recognition, *viz.* of identifying the right answer to a question.

In the beginning of the dialogue, Socrates explains what he expects
Meno to do in order to give him a single definition of *arete*: there is one
single *eidos* whereby all excellences are excellences, and it is by keeping it in view that one should answer the question 'What is human
excellence?' Socrates wants Meno to answer himself. When Meno
brings up opinions of others, such as his teacher Gorgias, Socrates
forces him to dismiss them as inadequate and would eventually have
him admit his ignorance. But, according to Meno's understanding of
the learning situation, admission of ignorance, on the terms set by
Socrates, far from being a necessary condition of inquiry, totally prevents it. Socrates' method puts the interlocutor in an impossible situation; it brings him to a realization of his ignorance, i.e. of his not
having the knowledge sought, and then asks him to search for that
knowledge within himself.

On Meno's view, the first requisite for learning is a good memory,
such as Meno himself has.[1] His suggested definitions of virtue are all
quoted, with acknowledgments, first from Gorgias (71 E, 73 C), then
from an unnamed poet (77 B2). Indeed, the development of a good
memory was a main tenet of sophistic education; Gorgias' oratoric
set-pieces may have been intended to be learned by heart, and
Hippias is said to have developed a 'mnemonic technique' and himself to have had a prodigious memory.[2] On such a view, to be able to
answer a question is to be able to pick up the right answer from among
the pieces of information one has committed to one's soul – or, in
more modern terminology, from one's 'repertory' of (verbal)
responses.

For Meno, there is a clean cut between knowledge and ignorance.
In this he is following Parmenides, who first postulated an unbridge-
able gap between being and not being and a parallel dichotomy between knowing and not knowing. There are no intermediate stages;
either the information sought is there or it isn't.[3] The passage from
ignorance to knowledge must be instantaneous, but it cannot be
accomplished by the soul's own resources. One cannot find the
answer by looking, as it were, inside oneself, unless the desired information is already there. Moreover, the only way knowledge could
have come into the soul in the first place is by having been put there
from the outside. And this is what Meno tries to do throughout the
dialogue, to amass information. But this is precisely what Socrates
forbids him to do.

Socrates rephrases Meno's paradox, and in so doing he changes it
in some crucial ways:

> I see what you say, Meno. . . That it is impossible for a man to
> search either for what he knows or for what he does not know; for
> he would search neither for what he knows – for he knows it already

and there is no need to search for such a thing; nor for what he does not know – for he would not know what to search for. (80 E1–5).[4]

Socrates introduces three main changes in Meno's version: he adds the impossibility of learning also what one knows, while Meno objected only to the possibility of inquiry into what one does not know; he omits Meno's difficulty about recognizing whether the results of the inquiry correspond to what one was looking for; and he omits from Meno's formulation the adverbial phrase 'at all'.[5]

In omitting the adverbial phrase, Socrates evades Meno's Eleatic dichotomy. And it is this denial of the dichotomy which will enable Plato to overcome the dilemma. Before starting the 'geometry lesson', Socrates asks Meno whether the boy is Greek and speaks Greek (81 B4). This not only ensures the possibility of communication – a necessary but trivial point. More importantly, it ensures that the words that will be used during the interchange (and especially such terms as 'square', 'side', 'double', which are part of the everyday language but will have a semi-technical function in the argument) arouse in the boy certain associations which are more or less common to all Greek speakers. Socrates can assume, to a certain extent, a minimal conceptual world common to him and the boy, from which the inquiry can make a start. Indeed, the boy recognizes that the figure drawn by Socrates is a square.[6] He sees that the four sides of a square are equal and so are its diagonals.[7] He can calculate. Unlike Meno's question at the beginning of the dialogue, there is a minimal context into which the inquiry is set, and there is a minimal *Lebenswelt* from which material for the inquiry can be drawn.

Socrates' first questions gradually clarify the concept of a square, which the boy already had, but in an indistinct manner. The boy recognizes a square, but he has not necessarily considered explicitly whether its sides or its diagonals are equal. But once prompted by Socrates' questions, he can see that this is indeed the case.

The starting point of the learning process, as Plato presents it in this paradigm case, is in semi-explained, semi-understood concepts. Were the starting point absolute ignorance, we would indeed be faced with Meno's version of the paradox. As Meno has it, if one does not know 'at all' what it is that one is looking for, one cannot recognize the solution even if one happens to be presented with it. Had the boy known absolutely nothing about squares, Socrates' questions could not have elicited from him any answers, right or wrong.

But Socrates' questions show that this is not the case. One always has a minimal knowledge which allows one to recognize at least parts of the answer, even if in a vague and confused manner. The boy does not know on which line the double square is built. But he recognizes a square and can be brought to realize some of the basic relations between its lines; he knows what 'double' is and he can calculate; and he can be made to understand what it means to build a square on a given line. It would not be correct to describe him as not knowing 'at all' what he is looking for. In fact, as the geometry lesson shows, the correct answer will eventually be set, little by little, in the context of whatever the boy already knew, and therefore there will be no problem in recognizing it, as Meno feared.

Meno assumes that knowledge is atomic, unanalysed and unanalysable, and not context-dependent. Like Socrates, he too expects a yes-or-no answer to his question 'Is *arete* teachable?' But, unlike Socrates, Meno does not expect the answer to arise from an analysis of the terms of the question – which is what Socrates does in the geometry lesson, or in his reply to Meno (cf., e.g., 71 B). If the interlocutor cannot answer the question put to him, the possibility is always open to Socrates of splitting up the question into smaller steps (cf. 85 A4–5) or setting it into a wider context by means of analogy (cf., e.g., 72 A–C). In other words, even in the case that the respondent cannot answer the original question himself, he will always have within himself the materials for a partial answer, from which further progress can be made.

The boy's first answer is naively obvious; the double square is built on the double side. His mistake is taken by Socrates and Meno as a sign that the boy is not being taught, but is answering 'of himself'. Socrates quickly makes the boy recognize his mistake; the square built on the double side will be four times as large as the original square, not twice as large. This is quite straightforward. But next Socrates draws the boy into a trap. Obviously, he points out, the side sought must be greater than the original side of two feet and smaller than the double side of four feet. The boy cannot avoid falling into the trap; the desired line must be three feet long. And when Socrates shows him that he is wrong again, the boy reacts emotionally: 'But, by Zeus, Socrates, *I* don't know!' (84 A1). Only then is Socrates prepared to bail the boy out and lead him to the correct answer.

As Socrates observes, addressing Meno, now the boy is in a better position to learn, for 'as he does not know, so he does not think he knows' (84 A7–B1). Of course, as long as the boy thought that the double square is built on the double side, he would have no incentive to learn. But once he realized his first error with a mild shock,[8] why did Socrates so carefully push him into the three-foot trap? It seems that Socrates wanted to make sure that all escape routes are blocked. The boy must be made painfully aware that, within his conceptual framework, i.e. within the domain of the natural numbers, there is no possible answer to the problem. He is thus forced to realize not only that he does not know the answer, but – more importantly – that although an answer there must be, for obviously the square can be doubled (cf. 82 D5–7), that answer cannot be found within the only conceptual framework he has. The boy's exclamation at becoming conscious of his predicament at 84 A1 is an existential expression of despair at the collapse of his conceptual world.

Internal criticism of the interlocutor's conceptual framework is, of course, a basic component of Socrates' method and of all Socratic dialogues. But only in the *Meno* do we have Socrates attempting, for the first time, to change his interlocutor's conceptual framework. He succeeds to some extent with the boy, and he fails with Meno himself.[9]

Socrates wants to bring Meno to nothing less than a full conceptual revolution. He wants Meno to realize that his concept of learning as acquiring information is totally inadequate. A change in Meno's concept of learning, of the type desired by Socrates, necessarily involves radical changes in some other related concepts, such as teaching, knowledge and ignorance, and the concept of virtue or excellence itself. As long as Meno clings to his understanding of these concepts, no solution to the problem can be forthcoming. But Meno refuses to go along with Socrates. He returns time and again to his old position; he would rather hear Socrates' views on the question posed at the beginning of the dialogue.

As Socrates points out, the geometry lesson does not prove conclusively that knowledge is recollection. But then he did not want to prove it. He wanted only to resolve the *aporia* they were in. The contention was that knowledge is impossible. Socrates had therefore to show how it is possible. In assuming the premises of recollection at 81 D, he does not say that from the premises something necessarily follows (although this could be the case too). Rather, he says that, granted these premises, *nothing prevents* the soul from learning. Socrates is interested in showing the possibility of the conclusion, or, in other words, in untying the *aporia* in order to permit a 'free way'.

As the 'geometry lesson' established, the boy did have opinions that were his own (85 D8–9), but, as agreed at C2–3, these opinions did not amount to knowledge. The distinction is important, for from it Socrates draws the conclusion that 'he who does not know about any matters, whatever they be, may have true opinions on such matters, about which he knows nothing' (C6–7). The geometry lesson has thus shown that the dichotomy knowledge/ignorance presented by Meno and by the two sophists in the *Euthydemus* is untrue to the facts.

True opinions are no less opinions because they are true; one may hit upon the way to Larissa without actually knowing it, perhaps by following a description of it or by trusting some intuition. The truth of *p* is presumably a necessary condition of one's knowledge of p, but it is not a sufficient condition of it.[10] Only recollection is knowledge *stricto sensu*, for it is 'recovery of knowledge within oneself' (*analam-banein auton en hauto epistemen*, 85 D6), as opposed to opinion, which is acquired from without. Knowledge implies the capacity of giving reasons. But reasons as such can never be given from without, for giving a reason involves seeing that the reason is a reason.

Because he is incapable of grasping the change of meaning that 'knowledge' has undergone in Socrates' explanation of the experiment, Meno still understands knowledge as something that can be acquired from without, and his concept of teaching corresponds to his concept of knowledge. Socrates, however, intends knowledge to be understood as recollection, and his concept of teaching is fitting to what he had just done to the slave boy. Plato refuses, for good dramatic reasons, to clarify the ambiguity, and the *aporia* of this dialogue will result precisely from his wilful play on it.[11]

In the 'geometry lesson' Socrates is content to show that the knowledge/ignorance dichotomy is ill-founded and that, as a matter of fact, it is possible to rid oneself of false opinions and eventually pass from a state of having true opinions to a state of having knowledge. If the boy is asked many times about these matters he will in the end have the knowledge which he now lacks (85 C10–11). This may be a long process. Plato does not seem to allude in the *Meno* to the questions intimated in the *Phaedo* and raised explicitly in the *Republic*. But if knowledge in the *Meno* differs from opinion by the possibility of having a *logos* of it – an account or a reason – then Plato sooner or later has to face the problem of the validity of a *logos* which is itself, as the *Meno* acknowledges, merely an opinion even if possibly a true one.

For a moment (85 D9–10), Plato indulges in considering the boy as already having made the whole way to knowledge. But at E7 he comes back to speaking of him as having only opinions, and at 86 A7 as having had 'true opinions which have only to be awakened by questioning to become knowledge'. Plato is not interested here in showing how knowledge actually arises in the soul, but in solving the *aporia* of learning as presented by Meno, i.e. in showing how learning is possible. Once this is done, the problem so far as Plato is concerned, is solved.

It should be noted that the source of the boy's opinions is irrelevant to the anamnestic process. The first solution proposed by the boy was probably one of his 'stock opinions', about which he had spoken, as Socrates jokingly presumed, many times before. His second, and wrong, solution was of his own invention. The correct solution was actually proposed by Socrates himself, which is perhaps rather unexpected, especially considering Socrates' sustained claims that he is teaching the boy nothing. But viewed in its proper light, this solution is offered by Socrates as nothing more than yet another opinion to be checked. As long as the boy accepts Socrates' proposal without checking it for himself, it is for him only an opinion, not different in respect of being an opinion (and not knowledge) from any other (false) opinions he had held. And although opinions (both false and true) can be handed over, the transformation of (true) opinions into knowledge, involving 'seeing' the connexions between the propositions leading to their confirmation, can only be done by the boy himself. His assent and his negation are solely his, and no one can perform them in his stead.

In this sense, Socrates is justified in insisting that he taught the boy nothing. In this sense, too, the geometry lesson was a demonstration of learning as recollection, i.e. of the passage from opinion to knowledge. But there is no continuous passage from false opinion to true opinion. Nor is there any question of 'approximation', unless one means by it that the successive hypotheses get 'closer' to the truth by some intuition or by Plato's literary design. But, from the point of view of the method, a false opinion is not gradually turned into a true one. It can only be refuted and replaced by another, to be examined in its turn. Since, by definition, false opinions are not part of the coherent cluster of truths (cf. 81 C9ff.), there are no logical links leading from false opinions to the truth. An opinion, whether true or false, is always irrational; true opinions, however, can gradually be set into a context of reasons. And this is recollection.

There is a difference between (true) opinion and knowledge, between those beliefs the boy entertained unreflectively and those he developed 'out of himself', as shown in the 'geometry lesson'. At the same time it was shown too that it is possible to pass gradually from (true) opinion to knowledge. This means that although opinion and knowledge are different from each other, yet they are not completely separate states; knowledge is opinion plus 'the calculation of the reason' (98 A3–4). He who has knowledge is capable of giving an account of what he knows, while he who has opinion only is not. By 'giving an account' Plato means showing the reason whereby a thing or a fact is as it is.[12] Knowing excellence to be teachable and believing excellence to be teachable differ not in the content of the cognition but in the ability or lack of abiity to give a reason for excellence being so. In this case, the reason proposed is that excellence is knowledge. *If* excellence is knowledge, it is teachable (87 B6). Of course, *that* excellence is knowledge is held only provisionally, as an opinion, until proved in its turn (cf. 87 Dff.). Thus, 'the calculation of the reason' can be done to a greater or smaller degree. Bare opinion is held totally unreflectively; absolute knowledge (which is not yet envisaged in the *Meno*) eventually requires the working out of the whole series of reasons. Learning is a process leading from a (more or less) unreflected opinion to a state in which the logical causes or reasons of that opinion are made explicit – mostly only partially.

Already at the beginning of the dialogue, Socrates asked for the 'why'. At 72 C6–7 he asked for the one and same configuration (*eidos*) whereby all the excellences Meno mentioned are excellences.[13] One may have a true opinion about excellence if one can enumerate examples of excellence when asked to do so. But one does not have knowledge unless one can 'think out the reason' whereby (*dia*) all excellences are excellences. Meno does not even have a true opinion of excellence, but, even if he had, he could not have gone much further because he does not understand the relation between the *eidos* and the particulars. He is prepared to accept at most a relation of subsumption, while Socrates wants a stronger, causative relation.[14]

Unlike Meno, the boy produced true opinions that were his own. He did not learn them in this life; he must have learned them 'when he was not a man'. And this Plato deems only possible if the soul is immortal.[15] Although the direction of the argument is from the boy's opinions to the immortality of the soul (cf. 86 B1–2), still the immortality of the soul is the cause whereby the boy has (or can have) true opinions of his own (cf. 85 Cff.). The possibility of the solution of the problem of learning is accounted for by recollection and the immortality of the soul. That it is the consequence (the actual fact of knowledge) that is important and that there is no question of an actual 'proof' is shown by Socrates' disclaimer at 86 B6f.: 'as for the rest, I cannot quite vouchsafe for the story'. It is not unimportant to note that here as elsewhere (e.g. 86 B2, 81 B5, and especially 81 D5ff.) Plato's ultimate conclusion is practical.[16]

Thus, one would be mistaken in saying that 'the nature of the difference [*sc.* between true opinion and knowledge] must depend on the validity of the theory of recollection'.[17] Plato emphatically maintains the former and disclaims any certainty about the latter (as he does again at *Phaedo* 114 D1–2). And yet, if Plato's procedure were dogmatic, setting himself to prove the possibility of learning and the difference between true opinion and knowledge from the doctrine of recollection, then such remarks would be true. But Plato's reservations regarding the doctrine of recollection make it abundantly clear that he viewed the conclusion as better established than the premises. If so, what did he need the premises for? The whole argument about knowledge and opinion seems to the point only if Plato was not trying to produce a synthetic proof of the difference between true opinion and knowledge and of the possibility of learning; however, on the contrary, he accepted these consequences from the beginning and was working his way 'backwards', from the consequences to the premises that would support them.

As we saw in the case of the boy's opinions, the actual source of the hypothesis is irrelevant. Moreover, if the hypothesis is the antecedent (or one of the antecedents) of an implication not necessarily convertible, then its provenance could be expected to be 'irrational', a sort of divination. As a matter of fact, anything could, *prima facie*, be taken into account, because everything is equally regarded as a provisional opinion until it is proved. Socrates can therefore allow himself to introduce his hypothesis as a myth, or to use an existing myth for his own purposes.

Now, the account offered in the *Meno* is irrational not in the sense that it is mythical – this could be only a literary device – but in the sense that it is a divination rather than a deduction. By clothing it in a mythical robe Plato seems to be stressing the non-deductive aspect of this account. This is the same aspect of divination that is implied in every regressive reasoning, and Socrates does not fail to mark it everywhere in the dialogues by tracing back the sources of his hypotheses to dreams, quotations from poets or straightforward illumination.

This squares well with Socrates' later disclaimer of the 'proof' of the possibility of learning, as against his emphatic endorsement of the ethical superiority of inquiry over intellectual laziness. Indeed, what is given is the consequence; intellectual courage is better, learning is possible (and therefore the dichotomy between ignorance and knowledge is spurious). For Plato, as he stressed so many times during the dialogue, the possibility of knowledge is a conviction, not primarily theoretical but practical. The first consequence Socrates draws from the assertion of the immortality of the soul is an ethical one: 'It is therefore that one must lead as pious a life as possible' (*dein de dia tauta hos hosiotata diabionai ton bion*, 81 B5–6). But the foundation of this conviction is something that he can only propose as a hypothesis, not guarantee as truth.

CHAPTER 8

Recollection revisited: *Theaetetus*

The *Theaetetus* picks up again the examination of memory, recollection and knowledge, and tries to differentiate between Plato's own conception of them and the conception based on current assumptions.[1] Up to a certain point, it is possible to understand Plato's concept of recollection from a dichotomic point of view, not unlike Meno's. But in this dialogue Plato shows that his new conception of knowledge and learning require a complete revision in common-sense metaphysical presuppositions, and especially in the concept of a unity.

It seems a quite straightforward assumption that either there are no perceptual or conceptual units or else that such units exist. In the first case, one could not refer back to a perception or to a concept, and memory and language would be impossible. One is thus led to the second possibility; since knowledge and learning require memory, one must assume perceptual and conceptual units. But on this assumption too knowledge is shown to be impossible.

As any other aporetic dialogue, the *Theaetetus* must be understood dialectically, i.e. as restricting itself to well-defined assumptions and developing them, without necessarily accepting them, but only in order to examine and eventually overthrow them. The Eleatic conclusion would have been that, since knowledge is impossible on either hypothesis, and the hypotheses are presumed mutually exclusive and jointly exhaustive, knowledge must be impossible. On such conditions, not even Plato's concept of recollection would be of help. However, in the *Theaetetus* Plato was not trying to say what knowledge is.[2] Given that there is knowledge and learning – a firm starting point of the *Meno* as well as of the *Sophist*[3] – the premises on which the argumentation was based must be revised.

The most famous of the Platonic characterizations of Socrates' role as a teacher is probably that passage of the *Theaetetus* where Socrates metaphorically describes himself as a midwife.[4] He himself knows nothing but he can cause others to discover knowledge in themselves. The thematic similarity to the recollection of the *Meno* is obvious,[5] but the similarity is more than thematic. An examination of what Socrates says about the maieutic process, as well as of how this process actually develops in the dialogue, makes clear in what way maieutic is the teaching counterpart of recollection as learning.

Socrates helps his interlocutors to 'give birth' to his ideas. This is sometimes taken to mean that the main part of the process is in the verbalizing of these opinions, somewhat like what happens at 151 E, where Theaetetus enunciates the view that 'knowledge is nothing but perception'. But Plato clearly points out that the 'birth' itself occurs only at 160 D–E. The formulations in the beginning and in the end of the maieutic process are practically identical, but the second formulation, although put in the same words, has a much more pregnant meaning for Theaetetus himself. It has been thoroughly clarified, and now Theaetetus' understanding of this formulation is much richer and better articulated than it was before. Socrates' midwifery is, then, not so much in encouraging the utterance of one's opinions (although it is in this too), as in their clarification, once uttered. This is the long and painful labour which Theaetetus undergoes.

The process of clarification of one's opinions gives way, in the second stage, to the development of their consequences and to the verification of one's opinions, i.e. to elenchus. As in the *Meno*, Socrates only suggests hypotheses (or propositions) for consideration. It is these suggestions that elicit assent or dissent, and it is only by assent or dissent that the suggestions become opinions (judgments). But, as in the *Meno*, the educational process can take place only if the opinions examined are one's own, i.e. if the interlocutor is prepared to endorse them, at least provisionally, or to accept them as consequences of opinions previously endorsed.

Another anchoring point of the interpretation is the interchange between Socrates and Theodorus, in the exact middle of the dialogue (172–177). As usual with Plato, this middle section forms a counterpoint to the rest of the dialogue.[6] In this interchange with Theodorus – who is very favourably depicted in the dialogue – Socrates contrasts the philosopher with those of the opposed nature. Whether or not in the course of it 'the moral Forms are plainly though unobtrusively mentioned',[7] the main theme of comparison is the philosopher's capacity to 'search in every way into the total nature of each of the things which are, taken as a whole' (174 A1, tr. McDowell). The theme of the 'whole' is the main theme of the description of the philosopher. The philosopher 'is accustomed to look at the whole earth' (E4), whereas those who lack a philosophical nature, 'because of their lack of education are not able to look at the whole (*to pan*)' (175 A1).

A correlated theme of that section is the anecdote about Thales, who incurred the ridicule of the Thracian servant for not seeing what was at his feet (174 A4–7). And yet Thales is the true philosopher, who 'strives to escape from here to there as quickly as possible'. And this flight is the 'imitation of God in the measure of the possible' (176 A7–B2).[8]

There is in the *Theaetetus* a discrepancy between, on the one hand, Socrates' description of the learning process and what actually takes place throughout the dialogue and, on the other hand, the views that are proposed in the dialogue itself as hypotheses meant to explain how learning is possible The meaning of the dialogue arises from the comparison between what happens in it – Theaetetus' learning process – and the purported interpretations offered in it and rejected.

One should, then, approach the *Theaetetus* as one should approach the *Meno*, bearing in mind Plato's own recommendations. It should not be assumed that in this dialogue Plato is offering an independent inquiry into the nature of knowledge or of perception. Rather, Plato is developing some assumptions about knowledge in order to show that these are inadequate to support what he could consider a viable account of learning and knowledge. Moreover, Plato's own central concept of *anamnesis* cannot be properly understood on such premises. As in the *Meno*, Plato is trying to conduct the reader towards a conceptual revolution, towards the realization that learning and knowledge cannot be understood on atomistic premises. On such premises, neither the distinction between opinion and knowledge nor the concept of recollection can be properly understood.

The alternative position to that of the *Theaetetus* is developed in the dialogues written about the time of the composition of the *Theaetetus*, viz. the *Parmenides*, the *Sophist* (which is formally a sequel to the *Theaetetus*) and the *Phaedrus* (written perhaps a little earlier). This is the position, already announced in the *Meno* and explicitly developed in the *Phaedo*, the *Symposium* and the *Republic*, that there are degrees of knowledge and that the passage from opinion to knowledge is gradual, and that the objects of cognition must be of the sort as to allow such gradual development. Accordingly, the *Republic* correlates these degrees of knowledge with degrees of being, and in the later dialogues Plato will argue that the objects of knowledge must be complex unities. The ultimate conclusion of the *Theaetetus* is, then, that recollection as the gradual transformation of opinion into knowledge requires a revision in the notion of what constitutes a perceptual or conceptual unit.

The *Theaetetus* assumes a dichotomic view. It is laid down[9] that either nothing is in itself one (153 E4–5), or else each thing is one (185 B2) and is different from any other and identical to itself (185 A11–12). What is not considered in the *Theaetetus* is escaping between the horns of the Parmenidean dilemma and assuming, as in the *Parmenides*, the *Phaedrus* and the *Sophist*, that things (including ideas) can be both one and many, and that unities can be, at the same time, complexes. Such complexes Plato calls, in the second hypothesis of the second part of the *Parmenides*, 'wholes'.[10] Indeed, if unities cannot be complexes, *anamnesis* and learning are impossible, as the second part of the dialogue will make clear.

The main question considered in the *Theaetetus* is, 'what is knowledge?' (145 E9). Theaetetus answers that 'as it seems to me just now, knowledge is nothing but perception' (151 E2–3). By 'perception' (*aisthesis*) Theaetetus seems to mean, at this point, chiefly perception of external objects. But the range of meanings of *aisthesis* will extend during the discussion also to the awareness of feelings, pains and pleasures, and emotions.[11] All this is in accordance with normal Greek usage. In the further development of the Protagorean position it will be taken to include not only each individual's feeling of 'hot, dry, sweet, and all of that sort' but also what each state considers[12] 'fine and reproachful (*kala kai aiskhra*), and just and unjust, and pious and otherwise' (171 E2–172 A3). When the identification of knowledge with *aisthesis* is finally abandoned, the alternative suggested is that 'knowledge is not in our conditions (*pathemata*) but in our reflection (*logismoi*) about them' (186 D2–4). Theaetetus' suggestion that knowledge is perception means, in its general form, that knowledge in the strict sense is direct, unreflected awareness. Or, if it is reflected upon, as may be the case of what seems to us to be just, etc., it is not the reflection that makes it knowledge, but the fact that so it seems to the subject, for whatever reason or for no reason in particular. The prototype of such awareness is sense-perception, especially vision, but the general epistemological thesis that direct awareness is sufficient for knowledge has wide-ranging ethical and political implications, as it is shown to imply a form of relativistic ethics (as in 171 E, quoted a few lines above).

Whatever one perceives must be true for him that perceives it. One cannot perceive wrongly: one can only perceive or fail to perceive. This is Protagoras' contention; each thing is for the percipient as he perceives it. The identification of knowledge in a strict sense with perception has a strong *prima facie* plausibility. As in the *Meno*, knowledge (*episteme*) in the strict sense is characterized as infallible and incorrigible; if I know p, p must be the case, or it is not knowledge. Perception appears to be the paradigmatic case of infallible and incorrigible cognition; if I perceive p, then my perception, in so far as it alone is concerned, is infallible and incorrigible. Hence, knowledge and perception can be taken to be only different names for infallible and incorrigible cognition.

'Knowing' and 'perceiving' are treated here as two-place predicates; 'x perceives F' and 'x knows F'. F must be understood here as the internal or intentional object of perception or knowledge. F is what is given in perception. There can be no independent object which is perceived. If the (supposedly external) object of my perception could be considered independently of my perception of it, then the question could arise about the correspondence of the content of my perception to its object. Perception would then be a three-place predicate ('x perceives the object F as G'). Such a view is developed in *Republic* V.[13] But in the *Theaetetus*, under the general assumption of the dichotomy between knowing and not knowing, being and non-being, such an understanding of cognition is impossible. Either one knows or one does not know; either one perceives or one does not perceive (165 B). Perceiving is seen as analogous to grasping[14]; one can grasp or fail to grasp, but one cannot grasp something as something else. See, for example, the difficulties that arise in the aviary model, concerning the possibility of grasping the wrong bird. Even there one does not see F as G but one grasps F instead of G. Similarly, on these premises, one can perceive or fail to perceive, but one cannot perceive something as something else. Thus, the content of one's perception is always true for him that perceives it as long as he so perceives it.

But if the (external) object of perception is ruled out and only the content of perception is to be considered, then nothing can be said to be one definite thing in itself (152 D2ff.), independently of the act of perception. Rather, each thing arises in the act of perception and is what it is only in relation to that particular act. Perception can be always and incorrigibly true only if there is no 'object' to be identified. Colour cannot be in the eye nor outside it – it cannot be anywhere by itself. We are thus led to assume that nothing is in itself one determinate thing (153 E4–5),[15] since it cannot be identified, and certainly not re-identified, independently of each act of perception; in each act of perception it comes to be something else. Only thus the problem of recognizing something for what it is does not arise and perception is always true. This state of affairs is to be contrasted with recollection and knowledge as developed in the *Phaedo* and in *Republic* V. There, recollection is the recognition of particulars for what they are, *viz.* reflections of the ideas.

The details of the elaborate theory of perception facetiously presented by Socrates as 'Protagoras' secret doctrine' (152 C–153 D) need not detain us much, as they have been thoroughly scrutinized in the literature.[16] However the function of that doctrine in the dialogue has not always been properly understood. Having assumed (*tithentes*) that 'nothing is in itself one', Plato is now bound to offer some account of the conditions on which this is possible. On Plato's account, then, nothing is in itself; being is always relative, or, better, there is no being, only coming to be for someone or for something (160 B9). Nothing can be said to be 'this' or 'that' independently of the act of perception. 'Subject' and 'object' are in themselves nothing but possibilities which can be differently actualized according to their different interactions. The 'object' is not only inaccessible apart from perception; it actually comes to be so and so in the act of perception itself, realizing itself differently in different acts of perception. This is the case with the 'subject' too. Properly speaking, there is no 'subject'; one can only speak of the subjective poles of successive acts of perception. There are no pre-existing subject and object that come together in the act of perception; rather, the act of perception is primary and in it one can distinguish two poles, the percipient and the perceived. But these are necessarily correlated to each other and neither is anything definite apart from its relation to the other.

Dreams and hallucinations pose no serious problem to this doctrine. On the contrary; if not even the subject itself is one definite thing and each perception is valid for the percipient in the act of perceiving it, then one cannot speak of the same percipient performing two acts of perception, but only of different acts of perception involving (necessarily) different percipients, since the percipient is 'realized' anew in each act, together with the object. Hence, there is no difference in validity between dream and reality. Each is true for the percipient in the moment of perceiving it. And thus, perception, being always and incorrigibly true, is knowledge in the strictest sense.

Here the maieutic process ends. What has Socrates done? He has not elicited from Theaetetus any totally new thoughts, except by way of encouraging him to speak up (148 C). This is indeed the first step in the process. But the chief part of it is the conversation bringing to the full explication of Theaetetus' position. Theatetus acknowledges the cogency of this explication (160 E4). The 'strange doctrines' introduced by Socrates during the conversation, such as 'Protagoras' secret doctrine', are not of necessity an integral part of Theaetetus' opinions. They were developed only for the sake of the elucidation of the question of whether knowledge is perception or not (163 A8–9). They have value only in so far as they can make possible the equation of knowledge with perception. There is no need and no justification in taking them as expressing anyone's views, Plato's or his opponents', in their own right.

To the identification of knowledge with perception Socrates raises two objections; the question of meaning and the question of memory. The first will not be dealt with in this dialogue as it lies outside the hypothetical framework of the *Theaetetus*. Plato deals with the problem of meaning in the *Cratylus*, where he dismisses the possibility of a theory of meaning on Heraclitean premises such as those developed in the first part of the *Theaetetus*.

The second objection is more important in our context, since the concepts of memory and recollection are central to Plato's account of learning and inquiry. The second part of the dialogue gradually develops a view which seems, at first sight, quite close to that presented in the *Meno*. It will become clear, however, that the interpretation of the doctrines of the *Meno* offered in this dialogue are based on a profound misunderstanding.

The Protagorean doctrine of knowledge as perception leaves no place for memory in any proper sense. On it, the man who remembers is different, in the moment of remembering, from the man who had the original perception, in the same way that what is now 'remembered' is a different object from that which was originally perceived. Thus, there is never memory or recollection but always a new perception. However, without memory, which provides continuity, there can be no argumentation (cf. 166 E2); in putting in Protagoras' mouth the request that they remember what was said earlier, Plato subtly undermines his Protagoras' own position.[17]

Without some objective state of affairs, there can be no expertise. Protagoras can rejoin, as he seems in fact to have done, that expertise has nothing to do with objective states of affairs but only with subjective states of mind. The man whom the doctor has cured feels better; his 'objective' condition, if there were any, would be irrelevant. Similarly, the educator brings the pupil to a condition which the pupil himself considers better, by his own standards. And the same is true of the legislator who gives laws to the state. Education will thus be change to a subjectively better state (cf. 167 A–B).[18]

One can try and turn the tables on Protagoras. Everyone says Protagoras is wrong in maintaining that each man is his own judge of truth and falsehood. Thus, he is obliged to accept their judgment of his theory. But if Protagoras could pop his head out of the ground he would have dismissed such argument as flimsy. Of course he thinks he is right and the many think he is wrong. But this is exactly his point. There can be no common measure of conflicting opinions, and in this sense there can be no real contradiction. To him it seems that he is right and so it is to him; to the many it seems that he is wrong and so it is to them (170 D1–175 D5).[19]

However, the knowledge of the expert has to do not with present states but with future ones. The doctor knows how it will seem to the patient in the future, while the patient may well be mistaken about it.[20]

Protagoreans could retreat to a minimalist position; in matters of the advantageous and the prejudicial the expert has the knowledge, but in matters of justice and piety and the like each is his own judge. The separation of justice from utility is, in fact, Glaucon's view in the *Republic*.[21] Plato does not raise his own view in the *Theaetetus*, except by way of pointing at it indirectly in the conversation with Theodorus, immediately following the statement of the minimalist position.[22] From an educational point of view, the question of justice and injustice is most important, but it can be adequately dealt with only within the framework of the consideration of 'the whole' – which is in fact what Plato does in the *Republic*. Already in the *Gorgias* the good was interpreted in teleological terms. In the *Republic* such consideration of the whole implies the doctrine of ideas. There Plato maintains that, in order to counter the separation of *nomos* and *phusis*, it is not enough that there be an objective reality. This reality must be such as to support a morality of *phusis*. Plato's full answer to the minimalist Protagorean position needs the idea of the Good as the guarantee of the moral character of reality.

Such arguments, however, do not take care of the view that present perception is always true for the perceiver. In this restricted sense, Plato seems to accept Protagoras' contention, but it has been voided of all non-trivial epistemological significance.

The first part of the dialogue yielded the conclusion that there can be no knowledge without memory. Unless we shut ourselves up within Protagoras' shrunken position, we have to acknowledge that the fact of memory implies recognition of recurring contents. Remembering something implies not only entertaining the recollected content in one's mind, but also recognizing that that content is the same one that was perceived or apprehended at a previous time. Phenomenologically, it also implies the awareness that the recollected content is apprehended as being the same content apprehended at an earlier time.

A condition of such recognition is the anti-Heraclitean hypothesis that there are things which are in themselves one and as such they can be re-identified in their various appearances. Thus, the second part of the dialogue deals with the other horn of the dilemma: there are things which are in themselves one.

The newly-introduced concept of recognition immediately raises the question of non-recognition. For Protagoras there can be no such question. Since all perception is valid in its own terms, there can be no false opinion. But if knowledge is not in *aisthesis* alone but in the assent or dissent following the perception, there is always a possibility that the assent or dissent is unjustified. Plato accepts, then, at least for the purposes of this dialogue, that perception is in itself incorrigible. But truth or falsehood, in a non-trivial sense, attach not to perception, or to some immediate awareness, but, with Descartes and against Spinoza, to the judgment or opinion (*doxa*) about them.[23] And opinion is in the assertion or denial.

Thinking (*dianoesthai*) is 'the conversation (*logos*) that the soul conducts itself with itself . . . asking itself to itself questions and giving answers, affirming and denying' (189 E6ff.). Thus one does not have an opinion until one asserts it, at least to oneself. That a certain content is entertained by someone does not yet make it his opinion. It is therefore that propositions can be put forward by Socrates for his interlocutor's consideration, while claiming (as, e.g., in the *Meno*) that the opinions expressed are not his. It is only his interlocutor's acceptance of the proposition that turns it into an 'opinion' or 'judgment'.[24] The real dialectical process is thus carried on within the soul. Socrates only provides 'food for thought', only materials for consideration. Without serious consideration of Socrates' sugggestions there can be no dialogue.

The wax-block model fulfills at least two not unrelated functions: it allows for non-present perceptions to be related to present ones; and it provides for some continuity of the subject, by means of memory. This model may be thought to bring us close enough to supporting recollection in the Platonic sense. On this model, however, impressions are registered on the wax-block only from the outside, and, as each impression is in itself one and distinct from any other, they can in themselves only become more or less clear or faded or blurred. But they are not intrinsically related to each other nor have they internal articulations. Thus, they can be substituted but they cannot be developed or clarified. An adequate explication of recollection is thus impossible on this model. Moreover, in so far as the wax-block model is still too much connected to perception, it does not explain how we can make false judgments about non-sensibles, such as concepts.

On the wax-block model, knowledge seems to be again an all-or-nothing affair. But recollection requires not only recognition: it requires that there be some kind of 'latent' knowledge, i.e. that knowledge be not only in the act of recognition but also, in a different sense, in a previous state of which one is not necessarily aware but which constitutes a necessary condition of the actual recognition. A necessary condition of the recognition of F is having previously perceived F and, in some sense, 'keeping' the memory of F, against which the new perception of F is to be matched. Before I know (recognize) F, I must know it in another sense, i.e. I must have a memory of it.

The model of the aviary takes care of these requirements. It introduces the distinction between actual and latent knowledge.[25] One may 'possess' knowledge without actually 'having' or exercising it. The soul is compared to an aviary empty at birth, into which pieces of knowledge are put as we learn them. Once they are there, we 'possess' them but we do not actually 'have' them until we recall them and exercise our knowledge by 'calling them to mind' or 'grasping' them.

The aviary model is an improvement on the wax-block model. The distinction made in it between two types of knowledge could not have been made in the previous model. The memory imprint on the wax-block is not itself knowledge. Knowledge is solely in the matching of perception to memory. Although the wax imprint is there before the matching takes place, it cannot itself in any way be 'actualized'. The aviary model introduces the crucial notion of actualization of knowledge. On the face of it, then, it is designed to account for recollection, for 'taking up knowledge in oneself'.

And yet this model too is insufficient. Pieces of knowledge are put into the soul from the outside. Each is one and is completely distinct from the others. As such, they can be recognized but they cannot be clarified or analysed. Each 'bird' is different from all the others and, in so far as they are connected to each other, the connexions between them can only be extrinsic and unexplained, mere associations. Socrates' description of the aviary does raise the possibility of some birds flying in flocks, and even some of them flying 'through them all'. This could almost have led to the Platonic solution (cf. *Sophist* 253 D5–E2). But, again, within the hypothetical framework of this dialogue, this suggestion cannot be pursued. If the flocks of birds are formed purely by association, they are useless for inquiry and knowledge, since following the connexions of the birds among themselves would not lead us beyond a description of the subject's psychological make-up, or else mere constant conjunctions.

On the other hand for the connexions to be intrinsic, the view has to be abandoned that each piece of knowledge is an indivisible unit. Take the case of $5+7=11$. Here, '12' and '11' are two pieces of knowledge. Each is one and is different from all others, and each of them is supposed to be indivisible. Thus, one can only grasp '11' instead of '12', as one can catch a ring-dove instead of a pigeon. The aviary (and *a fortiori* the wax-block) cannot take into account the relations between 5, 7 and 12. In the aviary, 12 cannot be decomposed into $5+7$ and 5 cannot be added to 7 to form 12.

This was what Theaetetus was doing for the irrational numbers. There seems not to be any relation (*logos*) between the side of the square and its diagonal. Any attempt to express both lengths in terms of each other is bound to fail. Theaetetus had found a way of relating them to each other, but not directly; sides and diagonals are intrinsically related to each other by way of their squares, and the same is true for cubes (cf. 148). Similarly, perceptions are related to each other, not only as constant conjunctions, but intrinsically, albeit indirectly, as reflections or imitations of ideas.[26] But this cannot be carried over from the framework to the dialogue itself, since it implies a metaphysical context which does not fit the dichotomy underlying the argument.

What one believes erroneously is not that $11=12$. No one would do that, as Theaetetus remarks (195 E). What one believes is that $5+7=11$.[27] But in the aviary model this belief cannot be expressed. Even holding two birds at once will not do; there is in this model no way in which the birds can be related to each other. I can hold '5+7' in one hand and '11' in the other, but the model does not allow me to express the fact that I think that the one is the other. I can catch one bird instead of another, but I cannot catch one bird as another. It is not the case that I think '11' instead of thinking '12'; nor is it the case that I think '11' instead of '5+7'. What I do is to think '11' as being '7+5'. But complex bids are excluded from the aviary by the hypothesis that 'each thing is one in itself and distinct from every other'. For the same reason, the few birds that fly through (*dia*) all the others remain unexplained.

Far from supporting *anamnesis* in the Platonic sense, the aviary model is markedly and purposely anti-anamnestic. Learning is putting birds into the aviary, i.e. acquiring information from the outside. The general assumption is that knowledge is perception or derived from perception.[28] There is recollection, but it is different from learning. Meno could have been quite happy with the model of the aviary. If the piece of knowledge being sought has not been previously put into the aviary, no amount of Socratic midwifery is going to cause it to be found there.

The change from 'possessing' to 'having' is abrupt and clear-cut. There are no degrees. According to the aviary model, inquiring is indeed 'taking up knowledge in oneself'. The interpretation offered is quite a plausible one; but, in Platonic terms, it is still unacceptable. The distinction between learning and recollection, which is crucial to the model, is the very distinction that was rejected by Plato in the *Meno*.

The root of the problem is in the quite un-Platonic assumption that there is a clear dichotomy: 'either one knows or one does not know' (188 A1). Even after learning and forgetting are put aside, since these have to do with acquiring and losing knowledge, not with exercising it, the dichotomy is still unacceptable. The Platonic conception requires degrees of knowledge. One can know more or less and one's cognition can develop from a less accurate state to a clearer and more accurate state.[29]

The third hypothesis acknowledges the point already made in the *Meno*, that true opinion is a necessary requisite of knowledge in the strict sense but is not sufficient for it. The hypothesis picks up the definition given in the *Meno* that 'knowledge is true opinion accompanied by a *logos*' (201 C9). We now have three different levels of cognition: awareness, recognition and interconnexion. Knowledge requires all of them.

This hypothesis recognizes that knowledge is not in the mere recognition of the object (for this could be true opinion) but in the awareness of certain conceptual interconnexions relative to the object of knowledge.[30]

According to this hypothesis, which Socrates presents as a dream of his, following up on Theaetetus' dream, everything is composed of elements (*stoicheia*), and in themselves these elements can be perceived (i.e. one can be aware of them) but they themselves have no *logos*; hence they cannot strictly be known. One can 'have' them or not 'have' them, but one cannot say anything of them, not even that they are or are not. They can only be named, but they cannot be said to be this or that. There is no possibility of attribution or predication. These elements form complexes and each of these complexes can be given a *logos*. Their *logos* is a 'weaving' of names which refer to the elements of which the complexes are composed.

At first sight, what Plato is proposing here is the same doctrine he proposes in *Phaedrus* 165 Dff. and in *Sophist* 259 E. How is this model of the *logos* as a weaving different from the doctrines of those dialogues, if at all? It seems that here Plato finally recognizes what was wrong with the aviary and tries to correct it by allowing complexes.

Here too, however, the approach is purely additive. The relations between the elements are purely external. The elements are prior to the whole and the whole is composed of elements. Can anything be a part (*meros*) of a complex without being an element (*stoicheion*) of it? Theaetetus, faithful to his premises, answers 'In no way' (205 B8–11). But in the *Phaedrus* and in the *Sophist* the whole is prior to its parts. In the process of division, or *diairesis*, the lower parts of the idea are not its elements. The higher idea is not put together[31] of the lower ones; these are parts into which the higher idea is divided, not elements of which it is composed.

Diairesis as described in these dialogues is a process of clarification and the definition is the summary and the product of the process of clarification. If one does not know 'at all' what angling is, one cannot even start the diairetical procedure. And, on the other hand, the concept of art which is at the beginning of the clarification of angling in the *Sophist* is not composed or put together of the concepts of acquisitive art and productive art. On the contrary, it is divided into them and is prior to them. The concept of the one which is divisible into its parts or aspects but is not identical with them, is discussed in the *Parmenides*, and put to use in the *Sophist*.

On the present assumptions, the requirement of a *logos* seems to be idle. If the *logos* is just a verbal expression of one's opinions, this is, as a condition of knowledge, trivially weak, and certainly not sufficient. Anyone who is not dumb or deaf or asleep can meet this requirement at any time.

A *logos* could be taken to be – again, on the present, additive assumption – an enumeration of the parts. But if cognition is assumed to be an off/on matter, to have true opinion already implies being capable of recognizing the object correctly, hence of being capable of supplying a correct enumeration. If the whole is nothing more than the sum of its parts, how can I identify an object witout identifying its parts? The same holds for the more sophisticated and economical suggestion that knowing something is being able to point out what distinguishes the object of inquiry from all other things. If each thing is one, and different from all others, then if one has a true opinion about something, this knowledge must imply recognition of the object and its distinction from all other objects.

And yet, in the interlude with Theodorus, Socrates had asked exactly for that; the knowledge of what justice and injustice are in themselves and how they differ from each other and from everything else. Furthermore, the dialectical procedure of the *Sophist* will yield an enumeration of parts, and, by such an enumeration, also provide the features that distinguish angling from all other arts. But there again the enumeration is not an enumeration of elements. Rather, the idea of angling (or of the sophist, for that matter) has its relations with other ideas clarified by its being more and more precisely located within a network of complex unities, each of which is one in itself but is at the same time divided into further complex unities.[32]

The *Theaetetus* started from an Eleatic dilemma; either nothing is in itself one, or else each thing is one in itself and completely distinct from all other things. Both horns of the dilemma led to impasses.[33] The Eleatic conclusion would have been, as Zeno had done in his arguments against motion, that the thing sought (motion, knowledge, learning) is impossible. But Plato's move is different. In his later dialogues, and especially in the second part of the *Parmenides*, he tries to escape between the horns of the Eleatic dilemma; things can be one and many at the same time. Only thus can knowledge as recollection be explained.

CHAPTER 9

The perfectibility of the individual: *Phaedrus* and *Symposium*

In the *Protagoras* and in the *Gorgias*, Plato had opposed the notions that each person is the sole judge of his own interests and that reason is purely instrumental. Against these, he put forward the view that there are objective interests dictated by reason and that, therefore, one could be mistaken about one's real interests, as distinct from what one believes ultimately to want.

For Protagoras and for Gorgias, as later for Hume, reason is purely deliberative, with no motive power of its own. As Hume says in a well-known passage:

> Nothing is more usual in philosophy, and even in common life, than to talk of the combat of passion and reason, to give the preference to reason and to assert that men are only so far virtuous as they conform themselves to its dictates .... In order to show the fallacy of all this philosophy, I shall endeavour to prove *first*, that reason alone can never be a motive to any action of the will; and *secondly*, that it can never oppose passion in the direction of the will.[1]

Reason is universal but powerless. All motivation comes from passion and it is passion that sets aims to the will. But passions are purely subjective, and so are all the aims of the will. Combat there may not be between passion and reason, but that is because there is nothing common to them: reason is calculation without drive; passion is thoughtless feeling. And only passion can direct the will. Reason itself cannot be a motive for action but in so far as it is instrumental to subjective emotions. Hence, all aims are subjective and no aim is better than any other. All this had already been discussed in the *Protagoras* and in the *Gorgias*.

In the *Phaedrus* and the *Symposium*, Plato defends his alternative view, that the dichotomy of reason and desire[2] is spurious; that reason does have motive power; that it does have aims of its own; that these aims are rooted in one's subjectivity but are also universally valid; and that, therefore, one can be mistaken about what one takes one's real aims to be, to the extent that these are not set up by reason. The desire examined in these dialogues is the strongest and most subjective of all: *eros*, i.e. love, and especially sexual love.[3]

The *Phaedrus* is composed of three speeches – one purportedly by the orator Lysias and two by Socrates – and of Socrates' critical discussions of them. Lysias' speech[4] is a set piece, defending the paradoxical thesis that it is better to prefer the attentions of a non-lover to those of a lover. No doubt, Lysias takes up this thesis also *pour épater les bourgeois*, but behind the display of rhetorical technique one can discover a serious contention: all desires are irrational, and love is exceptionally so – it is madness and it overrides all calculation. The non-lover is to be preferred, not because his ultimate interests are rational in themselves, but because he is in control of them. The non-lover is not overcome by his desires and is thus capable of organizing them with a view to furthering his own interests effectively. In particular, he will promote the interests of the boy he wooes[5] in so far as he is capable of seeing that the advantage of the other can be an instrument of his own advantage. For Lysias, as for Protagoras, rationality is the calculation of the most efficient way of achieving one's aims. As such, it is always preferable to unthinking emotion.

In his first speech, restating Lysias' views, Socrates is quick to point this out; Lysias' main assumption[6] was that the lover is mad, the non-lover is sane (235 E7ff., cf. 244 A5). It is clear to all that love is some sort of desire. But there are other desires too. There are in fact two sorts (*duo tine estin idea*)[7] which rule and lead us and which we follow wherever they lead. The one is *eros*, 'an irrational desire (*aneu logou . . . epithumia*), pursuing the enjoyment of beauty, [which] has gained the mastery over judgment (*doxa*) that prompts to right conduct' (238 B7ff.). Desire is here desire for self-gratification. There is no question of a desire to improve the other. On the contrary, one's self-fulfilment and self-gratification eventually exclude true self-fulfilment for others. Their advantage is contemplated only in so far as it can be instrumental to one's own interests. From this point of view there is no difference between the lover and the non-lover. The lover, seeking his own fulfilment, 'is bound to be jealous' of the improvement of his beloved (239 A7, cf. 239 E2–240 A8). But the non-lover does not delight in the other's improvement for its own sake; only, he can see, as the lover cannot, that the advantage of others may also be his own.

The other sort too pursues enjoyment of beauty (cf. 237 D4–5). It is a state of mind (*doxa*)[8] leading by calculation (*logoi*) to what is best. As often in Plato, the formulation is carefully ambiguous. Nothing is said yet about the nature either of this state of mind or of what is best. What is best could still be what is preferred on utilitarian grounds as commonly understood, the role of reason being then to make other aims subservient to it. That state of mind characteristic of him who is capable of restraining his other desires for the sake of an aim which he considers better than all others has the name of self-control or temperance (*sophrosune*, 237 E2–3). But Plato does avoid expressly calling that state of mind a desire. He leaves the door open for another understanding of the passage, on which what is best is what is so considered by reason itself. *Doxa* would then be the imperfect or insufficient perception of rational objects, as Plato describes it in *Republic* V, and the concomitant attraction to those objects, albeit at a lower level of awareness, as in the *Symposium*. But, on Lysias' views as presented in Socrates' first speech, reason and desire are antithetical; extremes of desire block the use of one's reason. Full rationality as open-eyed pursuit of one's interest is incompatible with the madness of desire, under which no long-term priorities can be established among one's conflicting drives.

In Socrates' second speech, Plato develops his alternative view of rationality. Socrates starts with the denial that madness is bad and soundness of mind, understood as emotionless calculation, is to be preferred. 'If it were simply the truth that it is evil to be mad, those things were well said. However, the greatest of the goods come to us by way of madness' (244 A5–6). He who values cold reason devoid of passion above emotional involvement is mistaken about the real advantages to be gained (245 A1–8). If reason is the calculation of one's interest, which can be chosen only by the subject himself, then one may be mistaken about the best ways to attain it (as the *Protagoras* showed), but not about what is one's ultimate interest. One may not be clear about it, one may not realize its implications, but one cannot choose it wrongly. If one's interest is empirically determined by one's desires, then Lysias is right, and the only question that arises is that of sorting out one's short- and long-term interests. In this case, one's perception of one's ultimate advantage is, in principle, incorrigible.[9]

But if there are rational emotions, i.e. if reason can itself have its preferences and its desires, then there are aims which are rational in themselves and universally valid because reason itself is universal. But then, if one's advantage is not purely subjective, one could be mistaken about one's real, i.e. rationally desirable, interests (cf. *Gorgias*). If reason does have its own interests, the height of desire is not of necessity irrational, but, much to the contrary, it may be the height of reason.

Thus, madness, far from being an evil, may be the greatest of goods. As usual with Plato, the conclusion is stated first, of which the proof is to be sought: 'What we have to prove is the opposite [of Lysias' thesis], namely, that this sort of madness [*viz.* love] is a gift of the gods, fraught with the greatest bliss' (245 B7).

The long 'proof' of the superiority of madness starts with a formal demonstration of the immortality of the soul, but continues in mythical form. As we shall see, the passage from the argumentative to the mythical mode is necessitated by the nature of the subject-matter itself.[10] Plato had already warned, at the beginning of the dialogue, against the attempt to reduce myths to mere allegories. Some sections of reality cannot be fully described in concrete terms or formally demonstrated, but only imperfectly pointed at, in an indirect way. The nature of the soul is a case in point. The nature of the sensible world in the *Timaeus* is another (cf., e.g., the decomposition of the elementary geometrical bodies into triangles, a procedure for which no equivalent in the actual world can be found).

As Socrates had just remarked, Lysias' contention, that the madness of love is not in the interest of the beloved and is indeed opposed to calculated self-interest, arises from a misunderstanding of the nature of one's real advantage. But only if there is an aim which is not reducible to empirical interests can one be mistaken about one's own advantage. That one can be mistaken about one's own real advantage is a fundamental assumption of Plato's (and of Socrates') ethics.

Plato does not have, and cannot have, a concept of value which is objectively and universally binding and yet independent of nature. Such a concept is tied up with the biblical idea of creation *ex nihilo*, i.e. with the idea that existence is supervenient on essence. The source of existence is also the source of value and it is prior to nature. Nature itself is not necessary, hence not normative. Values are external guidelines for changing the way things are, not, as in Greek thought, expressions of the way things are, ideally or in fact.

Since this line of thought is not open to Plato, he can oppose to the interpretation of value as empirical nature only a conception in which nature itself is not purely empirical. One still acts with a view to one's own advantage, but now this advantage is understood as not empirical but nevertheless as 'natural' in an extended sense.[11] The Greek view can be clarified by contrast to Kant. For Kant, values are not derived from nature but imposed on it. Kant, like Protagoras, denies that one can be mistaken about one's own interests. Only the subject himself can determine what is his own happiness. But for Kant happiness is not the primary end of moral action, as it is with all the Greeks.

On Plato's view, the immortality of the soul is a necessary condition of real self-interest not being restricted to empirical nature. For the real advantage to be transcendent, the soul must be capable of being attracted by non-empirical aims. And, indeed, reason (*nous*) is the capacity of attaining non-empirical objects. Plato's views on immortality are notoriously complex, and we need not examine them in full detail. What Plato needs at this stage is a non-empirical dimension to the soul. This dimension is represented by Plato as a temporal extension of the present life.

Plato's proof in the *Phaedrus* of the immortality of the soul is short.[12] It is presented analytically, as usual in Plato's arguments. The conclusion is stated first, and the premises are sought which will support the desired conclusion: soul[13] is immortal; that which is ever-moving[14] is immortal; that which moves itself is ever-moving; what moves itself is a principle (*arkhe*) of motion; the principle of motion is also imperishable (else all motion would eventually cease). But the being (*ousia*) of soul is to move itself and soul is the principle of all motion. Therefore, by retracing our steps backwards, we arrive at the conclusion that soul is immortal.

But what exactly is being proved? The Greek is inconclusive between 'All soul is immortal', collectively taken, and 'Every soul is immortal', taken distributively.[15] The argument itself seems to prove only that all soul is immortal. There seems not to be in Plato a proper argument in favour of personal immortality, as distinct from mythical descriptions and expressions of belief. In the eschatological myths we do have continuity of memory, which is a necessary condition of personal immortality as commonly understood, but the only continuity of memory that is argued for is that involved in recollection. That memory is precisely not individual; much to the contrary, it is the memory of universal ideas, common to all souls.[16]

Plato does not attempt to prove individual immortality. The leap from collective to individual immortality must remain unexplained, much in the same way as the passage from the nature of soul in general to individual character must be based on myth, or indeed in the same way as the very existence of a material world has to be mythically supported in the *Timaeus*. But Plato does not need here individual immortality. All he needs is that the activity of the soul be not restricted to her bodily life. In Plato's eyes, the condition of the transcendence of human goals is immortality, even if it be immortality of all soul, collectively understood. At the least, the immortality of the soul means that the soul has a non-empirical dimension and that is her true nature. This non-empirical dimension is mythically represented as temporally extended.

The first step in establishing the transcendence of human aims is the recognition of love as essentially oriented towards another. Phaedrus, in the *Symposium*, strikes the right note, although in a primitive form; Eros inspires courage and love of honour and by these it draws out cities and individuals to great and beautiful acts, beyond the straightforward furthering of one's own interest, even to the point of self-sacrifice.[17] It is the nature of the soul to go beyond herself. This Plato cannot prove but only assert and describe in myth. The striving of the soul for goals outside itself is a psychological fact, and as such it can be acknowledged, but not demonstrated. One can only ask for its presuppositions.

The *Lysis* had shown that there is in man an innate desire for completion, for the remedying of one's shortcomings. The aims of one's activities are not completely extraneous, nor are they totally intrinsic. They are what one lacks, not unlike Aristotelian privation. Therefore, the *Lysis* discussed the good as akin (*oikeion*) to the agent.[18] The final *aporia* of the dialogue points already to the later Platonic conclusion that human shortcomings cannot be adequately analysed in purely human terms. Man seeks completion, but not in what is like him, for what is like him is equally deficient.[19] His completion is in what is akin to, but different from, him. In the *Lysis* there is no talk of an ontological difference. And, in any case, the utilitarian framework of that early dialogue would not bear such talk. Within that framework one can speak only of a desire to obtain what one empirically lacks, not of a drive towards a perfection which is above the individual. The question about the primary object of love (*proton philon*, 219 D1) must remain unanswered, since no answer can be given in terms of purely human deficiencies. In the *Lysis*, as in the *Protagoras* and the *Gorgias*, the basic positions of Socrates' interlocutors prevent any non-utilitarian discussion.

The *Symposium* elaborates this characterization of the objects of man's desires as akin to him. Aristophanes' story has a serious core; Eros is love of one's own wholeness. On the one hand, this wholeness is not to be found in the individual himself, and, on the other hand, it is indeed akin to him; it is 'his missing half'. But that 'half' is missing only in myth; it is not an empirical deficiency. Men are imperfect, not merely deficient, and their ultimate craving is a craving for perfection; their real aim is beyond them but is still part of their nature (*Symposium* 189 D).[20]

The self-transcendence of the soul has thus two aspects, intellectual and emotional. Emotionally it is a desire for immortality, for being unceasingly what it is – not, however, what it is empirically and accidentally, but what it is essentially, or, as Plato has it, immortally. Intellectually, the self-transcendence of the soul is recollection, i.e. the capacity of recognizing that its empirically-given perceptions are deficient and of being spurred by these deficiencies towards objects of cognition which are unconditionally valid.

These two drives are in fact one. 'All human soul', says Plato, '*of its nature* is in a state of having contemplated what is' (249 E4–5). In its true nature, the soul is reason (*nous*). The being of soul is motion (*kinesis*). But this cannot be motion in space, except in so far as the soul animates a body. The lower functions of the soul, such as appetites and emotions, which cannot be understood apart from a body, are imperfect expressions of an embodied reason, i.e. of a teleology which must work through mechanical causes. But the proper activity of soul by itself is non-bodily, non-spatial activity, i.e. thought. Not, however, calculation of means to extraneous aims, but thought which has aims essentially of its own, i.e. thought which is of itself attracted to its proper, non-empirical objects.[21]

The non-empirical dimension of soul is for Plato a necessary condition of recollection no less than it is for him a condition of the objectivity of the soul's real interests. The drive towards wholeness and immortality, on the one hand, and recollection, on the other, are, at bottom, the same. Love is the drive of the soul to become itself. But the soul in its purity is reason. Thus, the self-fulfilment of the soul is its actualization as reason. However, complete rationality and objectivity can never be attained in bodily life. Thus, one's true self is not the empirical, individual self, and the attraction of the soul towards beauty, as towards all objects, is truly the attraction of the true, rational self towards what is intelligible.

Thus, all love is *per se* love of the intelligible, however inadequately grasped and imperfectly realized, in individual objects. And since individual objects never are completely intelligible, love of them is never love of what they are as individuals. The object of love cannot be wholly in this life and in this world.

Plato's *eros* is thus love of the individual only in so far as he imperfectly embodies some objective goodness. It is not love of the individual for his own individuality, for what he is. This, for Plato, would have no educational value, for there would not be in it any drive to change the object of love so as to improve him, to make him worthier of love.

Aristotle does say that *philia*[22] is love of another person for his own sake (*heneka autou*). But there too it is not the individual in his individuality that is loved, but the objective good embodied in one's *philos*.[23] In so far as it is the good that is the object of *philia*, Aristotle agrees with Plato. The difference between them lies in their different views about whether the good is inherent in the object of love or whether love is directed, beyond its immediate object, towards a transcendent good. And once a transcendent good is accepted, it makes little sense to speak of reciprocity. For Aristotle, *philia* is basically a reciprocal relation; Plato's *eros* is essentially asymmetrical.[24]

Even for Kant, what is an end in itself is not the individual in his pure individuality, but the humanity in him, i.e. that general aspect which he embodies. Hence the respect which Kant demands even for someone's errors, since it is always to be assumed that he who errs is nevertheless rational and there is always the presumption of some rationality in what he thinks.[25]

Only Christian *agape* can be described as love of the individual himself for his own sake.[26] God loves the world without any motivation whatsoever, as a father loves a son. God forgives the sinner not because of any remnant of goodness that there may yet be in him, nor because of any objective independent goodness which the sinner strives unsuccessfully to realize, but solely because of God's free-giving love of man. Forgiveness is uncaused – it is the disregarding of a transgression or a shortcoming which, by itself, does not deserve to be disregarded.

And here lies the educational point of Plato's *eros*; because *eros* is love of objective perfection, it strives to make its empirical objects better. It is not love of the object as it is, but as it is in its perfection, in so far as it can attain that perfection. Euthydemus and Dionysodorus were not totally off the mark when they said that Socrates, in wanting Clinias to be wise, wanted him not to be what he was.[27] Educational *eros* is never satisfied with the individual as he is; it always strives to go beyond him and to reform him. Christian *agape* can forgive, but, in Platonic terms, it cannot educate.[28]

As the objects of the soul's contemplation become more and more intelligible, so becomes her desire stronger, until the soul arrives at the real goal of all her endeavours, which was only partially understood while on her way to it – the contemplation of purely intelligible beauty and its imitation to the best of her possibility.

The aim of *eros* is not the fulfilment of the empirical self. It does seek the perfection of the self, but that perfection is to be found only outside the empirical self, in supra-personal, eternal objects. But the soul, for Plato as for the Greeks in general, is never creative. She can contemplate, desire and, at most, imitate. But she cannot create out of herself alone. The objects of her activity and her desire must be given to her from without. Nor can the soul make those objects hers. Being essentially activity, the mode in which the soul can transcend herself and make the eternal objects 'her own' is imitation, i.e. reproduction of the intelligible objects in a sensible medium, as far as possible, in discourse, in social institutions, in artistic or technical production. By imitating the ideas in the world, the soul secures for herself some sort of immortality, turning the world, or parts of it, into the products of her pursuit of perfection. Hence the productive and practical aspects of *eros*. The *Symposium* makes clear from the start that *eros* seeks to transcend the self by an act of production, be it physical reproduction, artistic imitation or educational and political activity. Physical or spiritual creation is the empirical self's manner of attaining some sort of immortality. Education, as the fashioning of souls and societies in the image of the ideas, is the necessary outcome of *eros* (cf. *Symposium* 210 Bff.).

Therefore, in contrast to the Homeric gods, *eros* is free of jealousy

(*Symposium* 210 D6). This creative aspect of Platonic love is the mainspring of all educational activity. It is the creative aspect of *eros* that accounts for the descent of the philosopher back into the cave in *Republic* VII. For Plato, political and educational activity are the same. Plato's state is basically an educative entity. Having contemplated the good, the philosopher goes back into the cave because *eros*, as a desire to possess the good, drives him to seek immortality in reproducing the good in the material world. Self-fulfilment can only be achieved in the realization of an independent good, concretized, by means of educational and political activity, in laws and social institutions and ultimately in the souls of the citizens.

In the *Symposium*, the ascent of the soul towards intelligible beauty is also for the soul a process of clarification of herself. As the objects of contemplation and desire become gradually clearer and more intelligible, the soul understands that it was those intelligible objects that were all along the real end of her desires and endeavours. As in the *Gorgias*, so in the *Symposium*, the activity of the soul cannot be properly understood without the assumption of a unifying goal. The *Gorgias* had already shown that intelligibility, teleology and unity are closely connected. The teleological activity of the soul requires the hierarchical organization of her desires. The coherence of the desires can be secured, so Plato seems to have believed, only by an overall organization of the soul.

But the soul's self-clarification will lead to the realization that her deficiencies are not to be remedied by the sole attainment of internal coherence. The soul's yearning for perfection leads to an idea of perfection which goes beyond the individual soul. It is a desire for *imitatio dei*, a longing for a completeness which cannot be given in the individual. Thus, self-clarification necessarily leads, for Plato, to the realization that one's subjectivity is in fact a partial and deficient mode of perception of purely intelligible, supra-personal reality.

In its purity and in its most general terms, *imitatio dei* is the attaining of pure intelligibility.[29] In the myth of the heavenly procession of souls (*Phaedrus* 246 Eff.) this is the aim of the philosophical souls that follow Zeus. The followers of other gods fall short of it in varying degrees. The love of honour or of great military and political deeds is also a mode of self-transcendence, albeit inferior to the love of wisdom, since it implies an imperfect awareness of the true nature of its objects. Such too are the artistic impulse and the sexual drive.

But the empirical soul is not pure reason. There is in it an irrational element of individuality and character. Character is given, indeed, but it is not wholly natural, nor is all of it empirically determined. Differences in character are a fact not to be explained solely in naturalistic terms of physiology and education. The myth of the procession of the souls stresses the non-empirical component of character, as does the myth of the three metals in *Republic* III (415 A–C). Character cannot be explained without residue as a result of natural causes, physiological and psychological.

The *Timaeus*, being concerned with natural science, analyses character in purely scientific, positivistic terms; character is the result of nature and upbringing.[30] From the point of view of a science of nature, that is all there is to it, and all there can be. On the other hand, the myths of the procession of the souls in the *Phaedrus* and of the choice of lives in *Republic* X (617 Eff.) stress another aspect, which may be termed the transcendental responsibility of the individual soul. Although the individual soul is born into a given life with a character at least partially determined by factors beyond her control,[31] yet she cannot shirk responsibility for her life and character. Not leading a philosophical life is a failure and one is to bear the blame for it, even if, as a matter of psycho-physical causation, one can explain it away. Callicles cannot help being Callicles, but he is nevertheless to blame for it and he deserves punishment for being what he is.

Different souls, then, call for different educational approaches. There is, after all, a place for rhetorical and educational technique. The sophists had stressed the art of persuasion, the psychological technique of 'leading souls'. Plato was keenly aware of the importance of psychological understanding for educational practice. An empirical (hence, for him, not fully rational) psychological theory is a necessary requisite of any theory of education. This is why books cannot teach. They always say the same things to all, disregarding the differences between souls. They cannot teach one to recollect 'himself from within himself'. Dialectic as an educational art must be personal and differential. It requires a guide who is able to lead the soul from where she is, from within her subjective opinions. But education is also the drawing out of the soul towards the recognition of the true rational nature of her empirical desires. And Plato denied that this recognition could ultimately be empirical. For him, therefore, no theory of education could be adequate which lacked a metaphysical foundation.

CHAPTER 10

Method and truth: *Republic* V-VII

In the *Meno*, Plato established the fundamental epistemological distinction between knowledge and opinion. The geometry lesson showed that the process of learning starts from opinion and proceeds towards knowledge, by a gradual understanding of the *logos*. This is what the boy does – he discovers why. And it is in this realization of the why (*dia ti*) that learning lies. In the *Meno*, the difference between opinion and knowledge was explained solely in terms of their respective intrinsic characteristics: opinion is unexplained, unanalysed, out of context; knowledge, on the contrary, implies a context of reasons and its object can be explained and analysed.[1] In the *Meno*, no explicit ontology was involved. In effect, the road to Larissa was used as an example of both the object of knowledge and the object of opinion.[2] Whether at the time of writing the *Meno* Plato did not yet have an ontology to go with his epistemological distinction, or had it already but chose not to let it transpire, as it was not strictly called for by the needs of that dialogue – this is a matter on which it is futile to speculate.

But sooner or later Plato came to the conclusion that the distinction of opinion and knowledge by means of their intrinsic characteristics was not sufficient to counter the epistemological relativism of Protagoras and the sophists. Mere consistency or even full coherence cannot, by themselves, be sufficient guarantee of truth. There may be alternative systems of beliefs which are equally coherent, and unless one of them has an ontological edge over the others there may be no reason, except personal preference or cultural bias, to adopt one of them rather than any other.[3]

In the *Phaedo*, recollection was said to be the passage from the apprehension of sensible things to the apprehension of immaterial entities. Sensible things 'remind' us of the ideas they resemble; when we judge two sticks or two stones to be equal, we are inevitably aware also that they are equal in one respect but not in another (say, in length but not in colour), at one time but not at another, to one person but not necessarily to another. In judging them to be equal, we do not take them to be the equal itself,[4] but only to be equal in a qualified manner. Knowledge, for Plato, is infallible and necessary. Sensible experience, being contingent and changeable, cannot supply the proper objects of knowledge. Knowledge is of 'what is', not of what is only in a certain way.[5] Knowledge is of eternal, unqualified objects; opinion is of the sensible world. But it is not immediately clear how the account of recollection as awareness of the ideas in the *Phaedo* squares with the account in the *Meno* of recollection as the giving of a *logos*.

The straightforward pairing of object and states of mind was sufficient for the purposes of the *Phaedo*, where it served to establish the kinship of the soul to the ideas, i.e. its immateriality and rationality, and, as a consequence, its immortality. But, within a wider educational context, this formulation is too simplistic and inadequate. Morality and education have to do with the sensible world and make no sense apart from it. And here the minimalistic Protagorean of the *Theaetetus*[6] could still have it his way; even if there is objective, non-relativistic knowledge, it does not apply to matters of good and bad, just and unjust. Morality and education are thus irreducibly relativistic, and philosophy as Plato understood it is useless, except as mental gymnastics and cultural luggage.[7]

In *Republic* V Plato re-examines the distinction between knowledge and opinion from a different angle, this time with a view to providing it with a more refined ontological basis. The argument starts at 477 B with a firm statement to the effect that opinion is different from knowledge. For the Platonic Socrates and his company, this point needs no arguing (cf. 477 E6–7). Knowledge is infallible, opinion is fallible.[8] The second premise is stated at 477 B10–11: 'Knowledge, then, is of what is, to know what is as it is.'[9] As usual with Plato, the conclusion of the argument came earlier, at B7–8: 'Therefore (*ara*) opinion is of (or about, *epi*) something different from what knowledge is of, according to the power (or function, *dunamis*) of each.'

The realistic presuppositions of Plato come to the fore in his assumption that all cognition is cognition of something.[10] For knowledge to have any validity it must be cognition of an object which is independent of the act of knowledge itself. But opinion too has a claim to validity, inasmuch as opinion too can apprehend its object.[11] In the mere apprehension of the object, therefore, there is no difference between opinion and knowledge.

Here Plato explicitly introduces his analysis of cognition as a three-place predicate. He had already done that in the *Meno*, but only *en passant*, and again in the *Euthydemus*, for a somewhat different purpose.[12] That the triadic concept of cognition first occurs in these dialogues should not be a surprise, as it is crucial to Plato's own distinction between opinion and knowledge. The difference betwen them cannot be in the actual perception of the object. This is made quite clear in the *Theaetetus* and, in a lighter vein, in the *Euthydemus*.

Now, knowledge is of what is as it is, i.e. knowledge is of a definite character F as being indeed that definite character F.[13] Opinion too is apprehension of something as being F. However, if, *ex hypothesi*, knowledge and opinion are different from each other and knowledge is of what is F as being F, then opinion cannot also be of what is F, for in that case it would be indistinguishable from knowledge, both supposedly being cognition of F as F. Since both opinion and knowledge are apprehensions of something as being F, but opinion is deficient in comparison with knowledge, the difference must be in some sort of mismatching between what the object is and what it is taken to be. Opinion is not a failure to apprehend; it is apprehending in a different manner, assumed to be deficient in comparison with knowledge.

Opinion and knowledge must differ, then, in that knowledge is of what really (hence, for Plato, always and infallibly) is F, whereas opinion is of something else, if some suitable object can be found. He who merely has opinion[14] takes what is not truly F for what is truly, i.e. unrestrictedly, F. Having opinion (as opposed to having knowledge) of something as (truly) F, e.g. considering the many beautiful things, all or some of them, to be 'the beautiful' (476 B4ff.), means that the object of opinion is not (truly) F but something else. It cannot be, however, devoid of any character; opinion is of something, not of nothing.

Opinion is not error either. Error is misrecognition or misnaming, apprehending as F that which is different from F.[15] Opinion too is misapprehension, but it is a very special sort of misapprehension. Like dreaming, it is 'mistaking the likeness for that of which it is a likeness' (476 C2–8). Opinion is apprehending as truly F what is not truly F but only similar to what is truly F. One cannot deny that, in a sense, he who has opinion does know something (*eidos ti*, 476 E6). If he identifies something as F, he cannot be completely mistaken, in so far as he has a true opinion of it. What he apprehends must, then, be F in a sense, although, again, in a sense it is not. What one apprehends in opinion must be called F with some measure of appropriateness, although it cannot properly and strictly be F, by Plato's standards.

'Then apparently we have still left to find that which partakes of both being and not being and which could not be rightly described as either absolutely' (478 E1ff.). Such is the sensible world. If the criterion of genuine F-ness is not being also not-F, then sensible things can be called F only if they are allowed also to be not-F, albeit under certain restrictions or in certain circumstances, *viz.* not at the same time, not in the same respect and not in relation to the same thing. The beautiful itself will not be ugly[16] but sensible things may be beautiful at one time, ugly at another, beautiful in one respect, ugly in another, beautiful to one person, ugly to another, etc.[17] In this sense, sensible things can be said to 'tumble about somewhere between what is not and what absolutely is' (479 D5, tr. Lindsay).

Note that knowledge and opinion are not automatically allocated different objects. The argument in *Republic* V makes room for four types of cognition, of which only two (opinion and knowledge) are explicitly discussed. The other two are considered by Plato elsewhere.

If we represent by F' what is F only 'eponymously',[18] or derivatively, and disregard the cases of ignorance and error, which cannot be properly said to be cognition, we have the following varieties:

(a) apprehension of F as F, i.e. knowledge;
(b) apprehension of F' as F, i.e. opinion;
(c) apprehension of F as F', *viz. dianoia*, or the mode of cognition of the mathematical sciences, which operate with sensibles while in fact dealing with ideas; and
(d) apprehension of F' as F', or the philosopher's adequate perception of the sensible world as described at 520 C4–6 and in the *Timaeus*.[19]

Opinion is thus inadequate apprehension of the sensible world. The philosopher too is incapable of infallible apprehension of it, since all apprehension of the sensible world must be qualified as to time, aspects and relations. But the philosopher can give a likely account[20] of it, which is not completely devoid of reason and which, because it is only a likely account, is adequate to its subject matter, not claiming knowledge of what cannot strictly be known. Returning to the cave, the philosopher will be compelled to deal 'with the shadows of the just', but he will recognize them for what they are (517 E).

Opinion is not mere error because its claim to be the apprehension of F is not totally mistaken. It is, after all, the apprehension of the ideal character F as participated in by bodies and actions. It is this participation which makes possible the transition from opinion to knowledge. What has been presented in the *Meno* as a difference between modes of cognition is here given its metaphysical underpinning. The transition from *doxa*, as mere unreflected opinion, to knowledge through the giving of reasons is deemed possible because of the degree of rationality displayed by the sensible world, and this rationality is given its justification in the theory of ideas and participation. Were opinions exclusively of the sensible world as such, this transition would be at best unexplained. But opinion, as the uncritical acceptance of what both is and is not as that which truly and unrestrictedly is, can give way to the recognition that the shifting characters of this world have their reasons in other characters which truly and unrestrictedly deserve the names that are applied to the sensible world only eponymously. And this, says the *Phaedo*, is recollection and knowledge.

But why should there be inadequate apprehension of the sensible world? If we have the capacity of attaining the rational objects, why is it that we fail to do it? It is not enough to say that we have 'forgotten' and are now being 'reminded'. Education, says the Platonic Socrates, is not 'putting vision into blind eyes' (518 B). But if vision is there, how is it that we do not see? If Meno were right and learning were a matter of acquiring information the question would not have arisen. But the geometry lesson has shown that it is not so. The difference between opinion and knowledge is not in that in the latter one has some information which was not formerly available.

In the central section of the *Republic*, the Sun, Line and Cave,[21] Plato tries, among other things, to explain how this is possible. Sun, Line and Cave are built progressively, one on top of the other; they constitute, in fact, one complex image. The Sun states that opinion is the apprehension of objects without awareness of their reasons. Typically, such objects are sensible objects, for those are, as such, irrational. But the Divided Line shows how ideal objects too can be apprehended without full recognition of their reasons. This is what happens in the mathematical sciences. Finally, the Cave traces the soul's ideal ascent from a cognition based merely on constant conjunctions[22] to fully rational and synoptic knowledge. Opinion occurs because the soul is looking in the wrong direction. Its attention is directed towards its objects as they appear, not as they are in themselves. Education is turning the soul away from the objects of appearance of every kind and towards their rational explanations and causes. It demands a full conceptual revolution or conversion (*epistrophe*). Once the soul's attention is turned in the right direction, the soul 'remembers' of itself. Once it is aware of what is to be sought, it 'sees' the intelligible connexions, but not all at once and not immediately, for one's mental habits are too deeply ingrained, sometimes ineradicably so. It is the role of the educator to try to overcome the mental habits of the pupil. As the earlier dialogues show, this is not always possible and it is never easy.

In answer to Glaucon's request that he give an account of the Good, Socrates declares that he fears this account to be beyond his powers and beyond the *élan* of the present inquiry, and offers instead to tell him 'what appears as the offspring of the Good and the thing most resembling to it' (506 D).

Socrates starts by distinguishing between the many beautiful things and the beautiful itself. Over against the many beautiful things, one idea is posited and is said to be 'what is' (*ho estin*). The many beautiful things are visible but not intelligible; the idea is intelligible but not visible. All this is familiar ground to the readers of the *Phaedo*.

So far, the distinction is the old one between the sensible and the intelligible. In order to make this clear, Plato proceeds to add hearing and other senses. But, having thus differentiated thought from the senses in general, he now singles out one of the senses. Although sight and the other senses are all alike in that they are opposed to thought, nevertheless sight is different from the other senses in one respect. While the other senses do not need 'a third' between them and their objects, sight does; there is no sight without light.

This is a strange distinction, and not only from a modern point of view. Plato knew full well that air is the medium of hearing.[23] However, Plato is not stating a scientific analogy but pointing out the simple fact that sight is the only sense which requires a medium (better, a condition), *viz.* light, which may or may not be present. Sound needs a medium, too, but (at least for Plato) this medium or condition is always present. And so with the other senses too. One may have the power of vision and colour may be present in the objects; nevertheless, without light nothing will be seen, not because of a failure of either the eye or of its object, but because of the absence of the condition under which alone the visible can be seen.

Now, the cause of this light which enables both our eyes to see and the visible to be seen is the sun. Socrates says:

> And it was the sun that I meant when I spoke of that offspring which the Good has created in the visible world, to stand there in the same relation to vision and visible things as that which the Good itself bears in the intelligible world to the intelligence and to intelligible objects. (508 B1–C2, tr. F.M. Cornford, *The Republic of Plato*, Oxford, Clarendon Press, 1941)

When things are illuminated by the light of the day they are seen distinctly; but when they are seen under nocturnal lights, the eyes are dim and seem blind and clouded. In the same manner, when the object of cognition is 'illuminated by truth and reality' the soul knows and understands. But when it looks towards the sombre world of generation and passing away, then it has only unstable opinions and seems without intelligence.

There are two aspects to Plato's distinction between knowledge and opinion, the epistemological and the ontological. The first answers to the demand for intrinsic transparency of knowledge as opposed to the opaqueness of opinion; knowledge implies the giving of reasons. The second answers the demand for the validity of truth as reality; truth is *a-letheia*, 'unconcealedness', as a property of objects.[24]

The *Phaedo* specifies the method by which the transition is made from opinion to knowledge, *viz.* the method of hypothesis.[25] This has two steps:

(1) assuming on each occasion the explanation (*logos*) which I judge to be the strongest, I posit as true whatever seems to me to be in agreement with this . . . and what does not – as not true. (100 A)

(2) And if anyone were to fasten upon the hypothesis itself, you would disregard him, and refuse to answer until you could consider the consequences of it and see whether they agreed or disagreed with each other. But when the time came for you to establish the hypothesis itself, you would pursue the same method: you would assume some higher hypothesis, the best you could find, and continue until you reached something sufficient (101 D–E, based on Hackforth's translation, R. Hackforth, *Plato's Phaedo*, Cambridge University Press, 1955).

The first step is in fact the Socratic elenchus: what does not agree with the hypothesis is posited as not-true; what does agree, as true. The basic relation is the relation of disagreement (*diaphonein*), i.e. of contradiction between the hypothesis and the proposition being considered. The relation of agreement is nothing more than the absence of disagreement; two propositions agree when there is no impediment to affirming both together.

Obviously, such procedure cannot ever give us truth but only the possibility of truth. Indeed, the verb 'posit' (*tithemi*) is used by Plato to designate the holding of some belief in a 'provisional and tentative' manner.[26] Thus, what agrees with the hypothesis is 'posited' provisionally as true.

On the one hand, this provisionality of the conclusion agrees well with the character of Socratic elenchus, which refutes propositions but never establishes them. And, on the other hand, it also agrees with Plato's conception of the task of philosophy as dissolution of *aporiai* and not as system-building.

The second step of the method deals with the hypotheses themselves. Here too the method gives us a tool for disproving hypotheses only. Those hypotheses entailing consequences which contradict the hypothesis, or each other, or other propositions worthy of acceptance, had been discarded. Other hypotheses will stand not because they are true but because they were not disproved.

Lack of disproof, however, is clearly not sufficient. The transition from a given opinion to its supporting hypothesis is no more than the transition from one opinion to another. Nevertheless, Plato says explicitly that the transformation of opinion into knowledge is achieved 'by the same method' (*hosautos*); by the laying down of yet another, higher hypothesis, which is to be tested only for lack of disproof. As long as the upward chain of hypotheses is not concluded, the reality of each and every hypothesis is never given but only postulated. Yet, the basic Platonic distinction which was the reason for developing the method of hypothesis itself – the distinction between knowledge and opinion – is tantamount to the requirement that reality be given, not merely postulated.

Hence the demand in the *Republic* for an unhypothetical beginning. The unhypothetical beginning guarantees that the chain of hypotheses does not continue indefinitely, and that at its end the reality is given which was until then only hypothesized. As the hypotheses are seen in their connexion to the unhypothetical beginning, they are no longer provisionally posited but fully asserted as true. The unhypothetical beginning guarantees that each of the hypotheses is in fact a *logos*, a true reason for the proposition it is meant to support.

This means that at the last point of the hypothetical ascent, transparency and validity, intrinsic explanation and truth, coalesce. There can be no full coherence or even full consistency without correspondence. Reality and intelligibility must be coextensive, or else true knowledge (*episteme*) is impossible. Plato interpreted intelligibility as coherence, as the teleological interdependence of parts and whole, as in the mathematical proof, in the biological organism and in human action. The teleological principle of the interdependence of parts and whole Plato called the Good.[27]

It is often said that 'Plato believed in the possibility of absolute incorrigible knowledge.' In itself, this statement is true, of course. But it is sometimes taken to mean that, for Plato, the starting-point of knowledge is an 'absolute incorrigible starting-point, guaranteed by an infallible intuition'.[28] Thus, the whole of Plato's approach to knowledge is misconceived and, from the outset, tinted with an Aristotelean or Cartesian tint.

Plato did believe in the possibility of absolute incorrigible knowledge, but this was what he sought to establish rather than his starting-point. He emphatically maintained that there is a difference between knowledge and opinion.[29] This difference could be obliterated; some sophists denied it altogether.[30] Plato would not deny it; and because he would not, he asked for the foundation that could guarantee such difference. His approach is pointedly anti-Cartesian. Descartes believed in absolute infallible knowledge because he believed in an absolute incorrigible starting-point, guaranteed by an incontrovertible intuition, from which knowledge could be derived. But for Plato there was no such incorrigible starting-point. Faithful to the Socratic approach, he would take his start from whatever happened to be the matter at hand and, from there, work his way 'upwards' toward the reasons and the reasons of those reasons. And, because he believed in the infallibility of knowledge, he was bound to postulate a real, absolute principle.

But it follows from the very nature of that absolute principle, as the culmination of the whole series of hypotheses, that it is inseparable from the chain of hypotheses leading to it. It cannot be fully understood in isolation or communicated like any other piece of information but it must arise out of the dialectical process itself.

The Line is a continuation of the Sun and a prologue to the culmination of the whole simile, the Cave. It starts with a brief restatement of the two fields (*topoi*) of the former analogy, the visible and the intelligible:

> Conceive, then, these two [*sc.* the Good and the sun], as we have said, one reigning over the intelligible realm, the other over the visible[31] . . . . Then take a line divided into two unequal segments and divide each segment again in the same proportion, that of the visible class and that of the intelligible, and they will be related to one another as in respect of clearness and obscurity. (509 D1–9)

Segment A in Figure 10.1 represents images, namely 'first shadows, then reflections in water or any compact, smooth and polished surface, and everything of that kind'. Segment B stands 'for what the first resembles, the living things around us and the whole class of natural or manufactured things' (510 A5–6).

In order to define the relation between A and B, namely between those objects that were introduced as copy and original, Socrates resorts to the ratio he has already established between opinion and knowledge: opinion is more obscure than knowledge but not as dark as ignorance; likewise its objects cannot be called absolutely real nor absolutely unreal, i.e. they are neither unrestrictedly F nor unrestrictedly not-F. Now, the relation between copy and original in the lower segment, in respect of their truth or lack of truth, is as the relation of the objects of opinion to the objects of knowledge. The previous distinction of clearness (509 D9 *sapheneia*) is now turned into a distinction of degrees of truth.

D

C

B

A

Figure 10.1 The Line

The passage to the upper line is well marked. And this is how it is described.

> In one segment the soul, using as images what were there reproduced, is forced to search from hypotheses, not moving towards a principle but towards a conclusion; in the other – she goes from hypotheses towards an unhypothetical beginning[32] without the images of the other segment, making her way through ideas themselves and ideas alone. (510 B4–9)

By means of the upper line Plato is especially concerned with establishing the difference between dialectic and mathematics and making clear why mathematics, although dealing with intelligible objects, is not the supreme dialectical science. It is not sufficient for knowledge in the strictest sense that its objects be intelligible. As put forward in the Sun, knowledge requires, in addition, that the objects be apprehended in a certain manner. The Line elaborates on the Sun, and explains how there can be opinion, or opinion-like apprehension, also of intelligible objects.[33]

As Plato would have it, the difference between mathematics and dialectic is twofold:

(a) mathematics uses sensible figures whereas dialectic proceeds always through ideas;
(b) mathematics is forced to proceed from hypotheses to a conclusion; dialectic goes from hypotheses to an unhypothetical beginning.

Plato has been taken to be referring in (a) to the geometers' practice of drawing their diagrams in the sand. But surely this cannot be the point. It would be irrelevant, in the midst of a very condensed passage dealing with the relative degrees of truth of geometry and dialectic, to disqualify geometry from being a science on the grounds of a procedure of geometers which is irrelevant to geometry itself and which can be easily done away with. It seems rather that what we have here must be related to whatever deficiencies geometry has in itself, not to extraneous procedures of geometers.

It may be true that Plato does not tell us much about what the ideas are, but he certainly takes great pains to tell us what they are not. One distinction Plato draws again and again is that the ideas, as opposed to physical objects, are not sensible, not corporeal, not spatial (i.e. neither extended nor located in space).

The relation of being alike implies some specified respect according to which things are said to be like one another.[34] At least in one respect the visible square is not a resemblance of the square itself, *viz.* in respect of being spatially extended, i.e. in respect of having four sides, four right angles, etc. For, if the square itself is an intelligible object, one determination it cannot possibly have, by Plato's own specifications, is spatiality. The square itself, far from having four perfectly straight sides and four perfect right angles, has no sides and no angles at all. If it had, it would be sensible (*aistheton*) not intelligible (*noeton*).

For Plato, shape is always visible.[35] The dichotomy is complete; either a thing is visible, corporeal, in space, or it is invisible, incorporeal, in no space. Plato rebukes geometers for having to do 'with visible kinds' (*tois horomenois eidesi*, 510 D4), whereas their real concern is with the square itself and with the diagonal itself, not the squares and diagonals which are corporeal and cast shadows and reflections but those that cannot be seen[36] except in the mind's eye (*teidianoiai*).

In order to have a square itself that would 'look' like a square drawn in the sand, Plato would have to have another space in addition to, and distinct from, the space of sensible objects. But there is for Plato no space apart from the public, sensible space of corporeal objects, and anything that has a shape must be located in that space. Even when we imagine a square, our *phantasmata* are still sensible.[37] Geometrical imagination is not different, in principle, from drawings in the sand. It too is bound to be of a particular figure, and irreducibly spatial. The actual drawing in the sand is not essential. In the *Meno*, Socrates presumably draws diagrams in front of the boy; but Plato does not do so for his readers. And yet, when we, the readers, follow Socrates' reasoning, we do not imagine the square itself, whatever that may be, but we have before us a particular square, assumed to have sides 2 feet long, irrespective of whether we actually draw it on a piece of paper or merely imagine it.

Maintaining that the physical square imitates the shape of some other square (ideal or semi-ideal) not only creates the insoluble and unnecessary problem of the 'objects of mathematics'; it makes Plato incapable of distinguishing between the corporeal (spatial, visible, tangible) and the incorporeal (non-spatial, invisible, intangible), in the very passage in which he is drawing this distinction.[38]

If so, an obvious question is in order. In what respect does the sensible square resemble the square itself? The answer is, I think, equally obvious, although it is, as we are warned in the *Phaedo*, disappointing; the sensible square is a resemblance of the square itself in respect of being a square.[39]

But there is no reason why a square should be thought of primarily as a visual (or sensible) shape. Indeed, in Platonic terms, it is a contradiction that the purely intelligible essence of the square should be adequately expressed in spatial (i.e. sensible) terms. In other words, what makes the square in the sand a square is not the fact that it has four (perfectly or imperfectly) straight sides and four (perfect or imperfect) right angles. Similarly, what makes the number 4 a square number is not the fact that its units can be arranged in a square pattern. What makes them both square is the fact that they are both imitations or representations in sensible space of the square itself, which is the essence common to the square shape and the square number.[40] This is the abstract structure which can be variously expressed by the number 4 or by the square shape. We could perhaps say – although I fear this may look rather pedestrian from this side of history – that the square itself is not very different from what we would represent in modern notation as n^2. A good example, quoted with approbation by Plato, is Theaetetus' attempt at a generalization of the theory of irrationals.[41] I am not implying that Plato had some such formula in mind; we know too little about Plato's own mathematical activities. But I think it reasonable to assert that Plato was stating here that the essential nature of geometry is not spatial.

The mathematical sciences are all alike in that, having their place between opinion and strict dialectical knowledge, they 'turn the eye of the soul' from the world of the senses to the intelligible world. Because these sciences deal with objects that can be adequately grasped only by the mind, notably with the concept of unity, they force the soul to go beyond what is apprehended by the senses.

At 523 Cff. Plato makes the preliminary point that there are at least some data of our senses which are contradictory. What is wrong with the senses is that they do not give us the impression of, say, soft and hard as something distinct (*kekhorismenon*, 524 C4) but as something confused (*sunkekhumenon ti*). Unity, of course, is always experienced in contradictory contexts. Anything that is seen to be one is also seen to be many.[42] Every sensible unit contains parts, but the true unit contains no parts and is always identical to itself. True unity and true number are not to be found, therefore, in the sensible world. Arithmetic can be used in the sensible world, but its proper objects are ideal objects. And as with arithmetic, so with geometry and stereometry (526 Cff.). Geometry is 'the knowledge of what eternally is, not of anything that comes to be this or that at some time and ceases to be'.

Nor is astronomy the study of 'the traceries in the skies'. Although they are the most beautiful and the most exact of sensible things, they too are deficient in truth and being. For true velocity and slowness cannot be apprehended by sight, only by the understanding. I should not take it so far as to suggest that Plato was heralding Leibniz's differential calculus. But, in this context, where the sensible elements in the mathematical sciences are presented as 'reflections' of true number, it is not unreasonable to understand 'real velocity and real slowness in their true number' as referring to some abstract, non-spatial, proportion.

The same is true of harmony. Consonance and dissonance are not essentially a matter of sounds but of abstract proportions; certain intervals are consonant because they embody, or imitate, certain primary relations. As in arithmetic or geometry, no amount of empirical observation and experiment, 'stretching strings on the rack' (531 B3–4), can, by themselves, produce an unequivocal unit of counting or measurement, or explain why an augmented fourth does not sound as smooth as a fifth.[43]

When studied separately, each of these sciences seems to have its own subject-matter and its own axioms, each of them being a system closed in itself.[44] But Plato argues that this is only a superficial account of these sciences. A deeper understanding of the mathematical sciences requires inquiring into 'the mutual relations and affinities (*ten allelon koinonian ... kai sungeneian*) which bind all these sciences together' (531 D1–2, tr. F.M. Cornford, *The Republic of Plato*, Oxford, Clarendon Press, 1941).

It is not a question of Plato intending to perform the arithmetization of geometry and of the other sciences. Rather, it seems that Plato saw in the mathematical sciences different sensible incarnations of an abstract theory of relations.[45] Two pebbles, two sticks one of which is half the length of the other, the Delian problem,[46] two horses one of which reaches the other side of the stadium in half the time as the other, two strings tuned at the interval of an octave C'–C – different as these may appear to the senses, they are all but representations in different media of the same abstract proportion. This number or proportion is the cause (*aitia*) of its several representations, in the same way that Simmias is the cause of his several portraits, i.e. in the same way that Simmias' having such and such features explains why his portraits have those features or some appropriate transformation of them. Finding out the reality which in fact the mathematical sciences study means coming to realize that they are not about things that can be counted or stretches that can be measured, solids that can be gauged, relations between moving things in space or between audible sounds, but about abstract proportions that can be variously represented. Dialectic trains the mind to see unity in diversity. The passage from mathematical to dialectical thinking involves the realization that the same essence can be – in fact is almost always – embodied in sensible contexts which are otherwise totally disparate. A case in point is the realization that justice in the soul and justice in the state, different as they may seem, are but two embodiments of the same abstract structure.

By why should the use of sensory imagination in mathematics be linked to the impossibility of checking its hypotheses? Plato speaks as if there were something in the nature of mathematics that would force the mathematician to resort to sensible figures and to proceed from unchecked hypotheses to their conclusions, unable to check the hypotheses themselves.

Plato gives three examples of mathematical hypotheses; the odd and the even, the figures and three kinds of angles. Plato seems to be asserting that the only basis the mathematician has for his assumptions is his sensible intuition. The geometer posits three kinds of angles because he cannot draw (or imagine) an angle that would be neither right nor acute nor obtuse. Similarly, that such and such figures 'exist' he proves ultimately by recurring to his spatial intuition. (As in the case that at least three straight lines are needed to form a closed figure. I do not think this was necessarily the example Plato had in mind, but the general point seems to have been something of the sort.) And again, that numbers are either odd or even is supported by an appeal to an intuition that Plato probably thought to be based on sensory imagination: if to a collection of items that can be divided into two equal parts one more item is added, the resulting collection will no longer be divisible into two equal parts; but if to this new collection another item is added, the then resulting collection will again be divisible into two equal parts.[47]

The geometers take these assumptions as their starting-points, 'on the ground that they are plain to everyone' (501 D1 *hos panti phaneron*, A.D. Lindsay's translation, *Plato's Republic*, London, Dent, 1935), when they should take as starting-points what is clear, i.e. intelligible, in itself, not what is apparent (*phaneron*) to sensible intuition. Space and sensibility are, for Plato, intrinsically irrational. And in so far as arithmetic and geometry are based on spatial or sensible intuitions, to that extent they are unintelligible, although they may be, in a sense, 'plain to everyone'. What is 'satisfactory' or 'sufficient' for the geometer is not so for the dialectician. Moreover, spatial intuitions are, in themselves, isolated from one another. If geometry and arithmetic are logically structured, this is not because of their sensible aspect, but in spite of it. As the *Phaedo* made clear, only ideas can be logically connected. Sensible things, situated in space, may participate indirectly in these logical connexions only in so far as they participate in the ideas. But as this participation is never complete, so the logicality of sensible things too is never complete.[48]

In the mathematical sciences Plato found a striking example of how strict logical relations could apply throughout in a medium that is essentially irrational. The irrationality of visual shapes and of audible sounds nevertheless gives way, at least partially, to rational relations. Plato's explanation for it was that the real subject-matter of mathematical science is not the sensible given or imagined, but the purely rational, of which the sensible is only a representation. For this reason, Plato maintains that the same objects are studied by mathematics and dialectic. However the latter sees them as fully rational because its method connects them and their assumptions to their explanatory principle (512 D1). Mathematics, precisely because it is deductive, must assume these assumptions as irreducibly given.

In the *Meno*, the method of hypothesis could be interpreted in purely logical terms. Plato's description of the method as such is reasonably self-contained even without recourse to metaphysical apparatus. However in the *Republic* it is much more difficult to dissociate method from metaphysics. The two aspects of the transformation of opinion into knowledge, *viz.* 'the calculation of the reason' (*Meno*) and the 'turning of the eye of the soul from becoming towards being' (*Republic*), turn out to be intimately connected. The mathematical sciences show that the incapacity of questioning the hypotheses and the appeal to sensible data are inseparable. Doing away with hypotheses is also doing away with sensible data.

The importance of the mathematical sciences for Platonic education is not restricted to the formal exercise of the mind – although this is, no doubt, an essential part of their educational value. The whole of arithmetic and calculation (*logistike*) are about number and unity (525 A9–10).[49] But unity is always experienced as contradictory, according to the diverse contexts in which it is considered. Arithmetic, however, forces the soul to consider unity and number not relative to given contexts but in themselves. An understanding of the real nature of unity and plurality is a requisite of the true statesman and educator. The educator is to achieve unity in the soul, so as to bring its conflicting elements into a harmony, and the statesman is to organize the state so as to make it into one state and prevent it from collapsing into a collection of warring factions.[50] The statesman and educator must understand the true nature of unity and its relation to plurality, how they can be brought together in the soul as in the state.

The objects of the different mathematical sciences are reflections of one single type of object. They are so many reflections in different media of the same intelligible objects. The same is true of justice in the soul and justice in the state. To recognize justice for what it is is to realize how the different acts of justice or the different organizations of the state and the soul are embodiments of the same configuration.[51] Moreover, it is to realize that this configuration is prior to, and independent of, the particular acts of justice and that it is that configuration which makes the particular act or character just.

The mathematical sciences show what is the true nature of a complex unity, such as the soul or the state. Different as these sciences seem, they all deal with structures of abstract relations. As the later dialogues will spell out in detail, it is structure that unifies plurality. Hence, the soul is one and the state is one to the extent in which they are structured. Plato interprets this structurization as a hierarchy, in the soul as in the state.[52]

The Line was an analogy; the lower half is to the upper half as each of the lower sections of each half is to the upper section of the respective half. Although all the sections are marked on a single line, the continuity of the line plays no role in the analogy. There is in the Line no movement from one section to another. The movement of thought in the upper section is contrasted with that in the section below it, but there is no passage from the lower to the upper section. The line is continuous only as an anticipation of the Cave.

It is only in the Cave that movement from one section to the next is introduced. The released prisoner is made to go through all the stages in an ordered sequence. But the Cave is not precisely parallel to the Line. In fact, we are given in the Cave a double image. On the one hand, the Cave is analogical; the world of the cave is parallel to the outside world. On the other hand, the Cave presents us with an upward scale. These two images of the Cave correspond to two movements. The conversion from looking at shadows to looking at the objects that cast those shadows is analogical to the conversion from the cognition of the cave to the cognition of the outside world, just as the relation between the two lower sections of the line is analogical to the relation between its halves. According to this image, there is no continuous movement. But on this movement another is superimposed, *viz.* a continuous ascent from the lowest to the highest cognition. As in all Platonic myths, no coherent picture can be formed to the last details, precisely because the state of affairs that Plato wishes to clarify is not to be adequately described in empirical terms.

The Cave has to be understood on both interpretations at the same time. It cannot be read as a step-by-step description of the actual psychological processes involved in the acquisition of knowledge. Rather, it must be seen as an explanatory construction, designed to clarify the essential nature of the conversion from empirical to ideal cognition. Like the expositions of the genesis of the state in Book II or of its degeneration in Books VIII–IX of the *Republic*, the Cave cannot be read as a straightforward story; here as there, the related time-sequences cannot be assumed to refer univocally to historical or psychological series of events.

The compound movement in the Cave points to two features of the educational process.

(a) The educational process is an ascent from inadequate to adequate cognition. The upward movement of the Cave is parallel,

in general terms, to the upward movement in the *Symposium*.[53]
(b) At the same time, the educational process is to be understood as a conversion, a complete restructuring of one's conceptual framework, as demonstrated in the previous dialogues.

There are in the educational process an element of continuity and an element of conversion, and both have to be taken into account. On the one hand, the transformation of opinion into knowledge is gradual; it is the tying down of opinions by reasoning, i.e. by enmeshing them in a context of reasons. The wider the context, the closer one is to knowledge. But, on the other hand, the passage from opinion to knowledge involves a complete change in one's mental set-up. It involves seeing the cogency of the reasons that support the opinions, instead of being swayed by psychological motives, such as private associations, the pressure of one's social or biological environment or the acceptance of the authority of the many or the prestigious or the powerful or the clever.

The conversion is necessarily sudden and unexplained. To be convinced by logical cogency is an event incommensurable with being overcome by psychological persuasion. That someone should acknowledge logical necessity instead, or in spite, of psychological necessity, is not to be explained in psychological terms alone.[54]

That the released prisoner is made to make the whole ascent from looking at shadows to looking directly at the sun does not mean that we start from looking at shadows in a literal sense. We are like the prisoners in that we are looking at shadows and reflections: not, however, at what we take to be shadows and reflections, and here is where we go wrong. Like the prisoners, we do not recognize the objects of our experience as shadows and reflections, and take them to be reality itself. The Cave puts our cognitive states one peg lower, so as to make us understand our predicament by comparison to the prisoners. As the prisoners are to us, so are we to the true state of affairs.[55]

At the end of the difficult ascent towards the idea of the Good, the detached studies are finally brought together in a 'synopsis' (557 C1), in an integrated vision of 'the mutual affinity of these sciences to one another and to the nature of reality'. For, says Plato, 'the dialectician is he who can see the whole, he who cannot see it – is not one' (537 C7). This is Plato's answer to Hippias.[56] The difference between encyclopedic and synoptic knowlege is in its articulation. This articulation will be spelled out in the diairetical procedure of the later dialogues. In the meantime, Plato postulates the idea of the Good as the idea of the articulation of the whole field of knowledge.

A note on practical reasoning

In demanding that kings be philosophers or philosophers kings, Plato squarely denies that practical reasoning is different from theoretical reasoning. For him, practical reasoning is the grasping of the common structures of moral situations. But these structures are not to be inferred from the moral situations themselves. Justice is not to be primarily considered as it appears in empirical contexts, for it could never be adequately understood from these contexts alone, but only as it is in itself, prior to any empirical context.[57]

On his own terms, Plato is justified in maintaining that there is no contradiction between the practical and the theoretical conception of the philosopher.[58] The *Gorgias* and the *Symposium* have shown how my apparently individual interests have to be understood as derivative from the objective interest of reason, misguided or corrupted as it may be; what I love or desire is not loved or desired for being the individual thing or person it is but for its real, non-individual, non-contingent nature. The *Symposium* shows that the height of objectivity is not separated from the deepest subjectivity but is generated out of that subjectivity itself; subjectivity can only be understood within a wider non-subjective context.

Justice does demand an ideal, impersonal point of view. But Plato denies that justice so understood 'is not in the interest of any actual people' and that 'justice demands that we positively stop being human'.[59] Much to the contrary. Plato's disagreement with Protagoras is precisely over what it is to be human. It is not irrelevant that the question 'Whatever is man?' is asked in the *Theaetetus*. Plato definitely rejects the Protagorean individualistic view of man. To be man is not to be plainly empirical. To adopt an individualistic view of man's interests is to be less than human.

Plato's answer to Protagoras is given, e.g., in the *Symposium*. There Plato denies that the empirical man is the actual man. Individual man is not the measure, not even of his own interests. Plato's whole metaphysics is designed to support the view that one's deepest interests are not empirically individualistic. To say that ideas are not 'in' sensible things and that these are 'imitations' of the ideas and 'fall short' of them is also to say that the idea of man as fully rational and in possession of complete knowledge is not to be derived from empirical man but empirical man is to be understood and evaluated in the light of the idea. Concurrently, education is, for Plato, the conversion from being motivated by 'my' interest to being attracted by supra-personal aims.

CHAPTER 11

Virtue without knowledge: *Republic* I–IV, IX–X

There are in the *Republic* two main conceptions of the state. According to the one, the state is the outcome of conflict; according to the other, it is a consequence of consensus. The first is the view of Thrasymachus and of Glaucon. For both, conflict is the basic political phenomenon. For Thrasymachus, the state arises from the resolution of the conflict in favour of one individual (who is thereby defined as 'the stronger'). Thrasymachus does not consider the possibility that the conflict may be resolved in favour of a group of several individuals. On his view, conflict being basic to the social situation, it will continue, in principle, until a clear resolution is reached in favour of a single individual. For Glaucon, too, the state is a consequence of conflict. But it arises from a compromise in which there are no clear victors and vanquished. Since a Thrasymachean resolution is unfeasible and, on a broader view of one's interests, perhaps also undesirable to everyone, all agree to a compromise. This, however, does not do away with the conflict. Rather, it establishes a somewhat precarious balance, in permanent risk of disruption, as stressed by the story of Gyges' ring.[1]

For Thrasymachus and Glaucon, as for the sophists and the liberal view of the state in general, the basic unit is the individual. The function of the state is to regulate the conflicts between individuals who must share the same (limited) resources. Both Thrasymachus and Glaucon deem the individual self-sufficient, and motivated by his own interest. In so far as other individuals are envisaged, it is as objects of one's activity or as threats to the fulfillment of one's interests. Interests are seen as inalienably and incorrigibly private (and in this sense they may be assimilated to pleasure) and irreducibly different for different individuals. As the interests of all cannot be fulfilled at the same time, conflict is in principle inevitable.[2] And since in the typical case the differences are irreducible, the resolution of the conflict must be in domination or in compromise.

For Glaucon, on the 'social contract' view, politics is the art of the possible. Each individual would like to fulfill all his interests completely. As conflict with the interests of others makes this impossible, one must be content with maximizing one's achievements, i.e. with fulfilling as much of one's interests as possible in a given situation.[3]

The state is a compromise between the best (having one's way in spite of all others) and the worst (submitting to the others to the detriment of one's own).

The Platonic genesis of the city in *Republic* II (369 A5–371 E11) presents a diametrically opposed conception of the individual. The individual is, in itself, insufficient, even economically. Political association, reduced to its minimal conditions, boils down to the mutual dependence of man on man. The basic social phenomenon is thus not conflict, but interdependence and cooperation. The fundamental social unit cannot be the individual, since the individual is not capable of standing on its own. At the core of the Platonic state lies a deep community of interests, a consensus that is not the result of a pragmatic compromise which leaves everyone dissatisfied, but a veritable 'common mind' (*homonoia*, 432 A7, cf. 351 D5). For, strictly, to be a citizen, on Plato's view, is not to be accidentally and perhaps also unwillingly trapped in a net of social and economic relations with other individuals. To be a citizen is to be part of the civic consensus. But it is a civic consensus, i.e. it is a common view concerning the establishment of the city itself. The content of this primary consensus is none other than the structure of the social group. The members of the embryonic city recognize each and all their individual insufficiency and their interdependence. Thus, for Plato, the real social and political unit is not the individual, but the social group as a whole, in so far as there is in it recognition of the mutual interest. In fact, it is the recognition of interdependence and mutual interest that defines the city as a political unit. For the other cities are each not one city but many (422 E–423 A, 462, 432 A).

Thus, for Plato, politics is not the art of regulating conflicts[4] but the art of making better citizens. The political aim of education is to promote *homonoia*, the political consensus without which no real state, as Plato understood it, can exist. Education aims at making people abler to participate in the community of mind formative of the city. Political consensus is not a 'by-product of the just life for all members of society'[5]; it is the chief necessary condition of it.

And, on the other hand, as Plato argued in the *Lysis* and in the *Symposium*, individual man is both deficient and imperfect.[6] The 'city of pigs' in *Republic* II cares for the economic deficiency of man. But, as Glaucon remarks (372), man's wants are not fulfilled by the satisfaction of his economic necessities. Man has desires which go beyond his immediate needs. They start with couches, sweets, perfumes and courtesans, but they go through art and music all the way to philosophy.

There is here a metaphysical point too. On Plato's view, the sophists were wrong about the nature of unity. They assumed that the state cannot be a real, natural unity. Only individuals can be the units of political association, the elements of which the state is put together. Plato's metaphysics is meant to show how the state, although complex, can be a real unity, and not only an artificial aggregate of individuals as indivisible units of interest and power. And as *Republic* IV will show, individual man is himself a complex unity of wants and desires of different sorts. The unity of the individual is in no way more obvious than the unity of the state. Both are composed of parts and both may or may not be properly unified.

Plato's politics, one may say, were in the main, Pythagorean; soul, city and cosmos are built according to one structure, and only he who has grasped that structure is qualified to lead the city. But it is not only a matter of understanding, or contemplating, that ideal structure. For Plato, following in Socrates' footsteps, there is no purely intellectual understanding. Reason is not pure light without heat. All understanding involves also a restructuring of the whole soul, cognitive as well as emotional. This restructuring is possible in Platonic terms because ultimately reason and passion are not seen as separate, conflicting elements in the soul (its *prima facie* tripartition notwithstanding),[7] but the degrees of knowledge provide at the same time also a gradation of clarity and adequacy of emotions.[8] As the *Symposium* teaches us, the height of intellectual achievement is also the summit of passion, consciously directed at the most adequate of objects. This basic inseparability of reason and passion can nevertheless be disrupted as, for example, in the corrupted philosophical natures described in the *Republic* 490 Eff. and so vividly brought to life in the portrait of Callicles in the *Gorgias*. But it is the common root of reason and passion that provides Plato with the answer to the Socratic problem of the weakness of the will and accounts for the educative power of the elenchus.

Plato learned from Socrates that the restructuring of the soul can come about only by a strenuous effort of self-examination and self-education. Socrates had left Plato in a real *aporia*. On the one hand, education, including political education, had to be differential and aimed at the attainment of a well-structured soul; and on this view of the soul, knowledge held a crucial place. On the other hand, no political educator can neglect the masses, which are incapable of philosophy (cf. 494 A4).

But Plato also learned from Socrates' failures. He could appreciate Socrates' point in letting go of Euthyphro and of Laches and of Meno in no better state of education than they had been before Socrates got hold of them. But he saw well enough that no city could be led on such premises. There is no denying that most of the so-called 'Socratic' dialogues of Plato come to nothing. One can clearly see in the end of the *Euthydemus*, for example, how keenly aware Plato was of the double-edged limitations of Socrates' methods, and how ambiguously he himself felt over those methods. (Xenophon's Socrates, by contrast, hardly ever fails.) Plato's concept of opinion enabled him to surmount what he saw as one of Socrates' most crippling political shortcomings, namely his incapacity of dealing with non-philosophical natures.

The Pythagorean doctrine of the tripartite soul (if Pythagorean it was) provided one part of Plato's solution to this dilemma. Plato's own anti-Parmenidean doctrine of degrees of knowledge supplied the other part. The doctrines of degrees of knowledge and of the three parts or aspects of the soul come together in Plato's concept of the soul as a unified structure of knowledge and emotion. It seems that the specifically non-Socratic trait in Plato's theory of the soul is the explication of, and the emphasis laid on, the incompletely rational, i.e. emotion and opinion. Socrates' elenchus dealt directly and forcefully with the irrational, or rather the semi-rational or quasi-rational, aspects of man. But the recognition of the educational importance of such aspects is at most only implicit. Socrates did not seem to have had an explicit theory of emotion or of opinion. Such a theory is apparently Platonic.

From an educational point of view, the theory of degrees of knowledge and emotion enabled Plato to do what Socrates could not and would not have done: to accept the relative value of right opinion in so far as it may approximate knowledge by degrees, without being in fact knowledge; and, by the same token, to accept the relative value of right emotion, in so far as it is the appropriate reaction of the soul to the right objects, although somewhat confused and not fully conscious and adequate. And, moreover, if knowledge and emotion are indeed inseparable except in pathological cases, a state of cognition carrying even partial justification should bring with it a better state of the soul as a whole, the goodness of which could be commensurate with the degree of clearness and justification inherent in such cognition. All this, of course, quite apart from the purely civic and pragmatic advantages accruing to right opinion and adequate emotion.

However, Plato clung all the more to the central tenet of Socrates' educational thought; human excellence or virtue (*arete*) is knowledge (*episteme*) or wisdom (*sophia*), but not of the technical kind taught by the sophists. As the *Hippias Minor* argued, it could not possibly be completely analogous to the other crafts, or it would have to be indifferent to matters of good and evil. For Plato, *sophia* was in essence the attainment of the unhypothetical beginning and the synoptic knowledge that followed from it. And for him too, not less than for Socrates, *sophia* could be achieved only by a personal effort, and by a long way. For Plato, as for Socrates, there were no short-cuts to virtue.

In Plato too, reason is supreme. But now reason rules not only in the soul but also in the state. In this last, reason is either present in the ruler who has attained *sophia* (as in the *Republic*) or in the law (as in the *Statesman*). Thus, submission to the philosopher-ruler, if indeed such a one can be found (and Plato is very doubtful it can, only the more so after his Syracusan misadventures), or submission to the law, is submission to reason. As such, it is valuable even when not fully understood, in the same way that *sophrosune* is laudable as being a reflection of *sophia* in the lower parts of the soul without being in fact *sophia*.

Socrates' failures brought Plato to the realization that his master's educational method could be applied only in exceptional cases. For Socrates, opinion, even true opinion, was valueless. The *Meno* introduced the epistemological value of true opinion as a practical guide (which was something Meno could appreciate), but even more as the starting-point of every learning process (which was beyond Meno's grasp). The *Republic* stresses its educational and political value, as a second best, for the many who cannot attain full knowledge. But, for all its value, opinion is still deficient.

For Socrates, philosophy was a matter of questioning one's beliefs. But in the *Republic* Plato could be construed as maintaining that having the right beliefs matters more than holding one's own beliefs, as a result of one's own thinking.[9] Plato does not renege on Socrates' ethical goal; but Plato, not less than Socrates, was keenly aware that few, if any, can attain that goal.[10] Even Socrates could not bring Euthyphro or Meno to anything. Plato, however, unlike Socrates, was unwilling to let go of those who could not be brought fully up to his standards. The best is that the individual rule himself 'from within'. But, faced with the choice between misrule and rule 'from without', Plato was bound to choose the second:

> Not that we agree with the opinion Thrasymachus had of the governed, and suppose that the slave ought to be ruled to his hurt, but we think that it is better for every man to be ruled by divinity and insight? It is best, of course, when he possesses that within him, but if he does not, it had better be put over him from without, and then all men, being guided by the same principle, will be equals and friends as far as may be. (590 D)

There is in the Socratic-Platonic concept of learning a tension between conviction and truth. Socrates took Protagoras' point that personal psychological conviction is a necessary condition of learning. But, whereas Protagoras considered it also a sufficient criterion of truth, Socrates would stubbornly maintain that there is a real difference between truth and falsehood and between good and bad, which is not dissoluble into psychological conviction, and that the degree of personal certainty is not, in itself, a guarantee of truth.[11]

Moreover, for Plato, philosophy does not establish the truth: it finds reasons for it. Platonic dialectic is not constructive. It either refutes untenable propositions or links unrefuted propositions[12] to their higher *logoi*. One's basic assumptions have to be given beforehand. True opinions have to precede the dialectical inquiry. Now, Plato takes it as a fact of political life that not all are capable of dialectical inquiry, certainly not of attaining the idea of the Good, which alone can give the full justification of true opinions. Until the idea of the Good is attained, there can be no definite decision in favour of the Socratic as against the Thrasymachean point of view. For those who cannot make it to the end of the road, all-out inquiry may be dangerous. Also, those whose intellectual capacities were developed in the wrong order, i.e. before they have developed the right opinions which are to serve as the intuitive starting-point of the dialectical ascent, may well develop an unbalanced personality leading to a purely destructive use of the intellect (537 Eff.).

It is not that the intellectual 'poses a threat to political stability' and 'intellect itself appears to be banished from the political arena'.[13] On the contrary, Plato wanted to reconcile intellect and politics, by making sure that politics followed from intellect. Inquiry is not in itself disruptive of the political order, but immature 'critical thinking' is not to be encouraged indiscriminately.

This is why Plato would start his education from gymnastic and music.[14] Philosophy will come at the end, not the least because philosophy is the finding of reasons for what we already hold to be true (and is in fact true). The lower stage of education, with its emphasis on habituation and on the formation of character, not only provides the moral base of education. It also provides the material for the dialectic which is to follow. From those virtues, instilled by music and gymnastic, reason is eventually to be distilled. However it can be purified from them because it is already there from the start; in fact, from the very start. Plato sees even in baby education – carrying and rocking, swaddling and lulling – the mastering of the internal chaos, the imposing of the regular movements of reason on the irregular motions of the Platonic equivalent of matter.[15] The failure to instil reason by degrees in the whole soul, even through its lower faculties, gives rise to the misology of *Phaedo* 89 C–D and *Republic* 411 D.

Rationality will not appear of itself. It must be developed gradually out of the irrational and the semi-rational. Knowledge can be formed only from opinions, and fully conscious virtue, or virtue as knowledge, can come only out of habituation and the unconscious possession of a virtuous character.[16] This is, in effect, the educational and psychological counterpart of the Platonic method of hypothesis and of his conception of philosophy.[17]

The most elementary education is to ensure a 'community of pleasure and pain' (464). Conflict arises from the diversity of people's interests. Archilochus, in the seventh century BC, had already remarked on it: 'But of different men the heart is pleased differently.'[18] If the citizens could rejoice in the same things, they would indeed form one body. So far Plato acknowledges Protagoras' point. Plato grants that pleasure, in its broader sense, is a powerful motive. But Plato's citizens are not to be brought up to any arbitrary object of pleasure and identification, such as ethnic values or national culture or a particular way of life. They are to be brought up to rejoice in reason, even in its lowest forms – regular movements, popular virtue, harmony and truthful myths. What Plato is trying to do is to instil a commitment to reason whose roots go deep into the unconscious and the irrational, from where reason is eventually to arise. But it will not arise if it is not carefully nurtured.

The outcome of such an education should be justice[19] as the internal management of one's soul (443). Justice is a matter of mental health[20] – it is primarily not a matter of inter-personal relations, but of relations inside the single soul (444). It is justice as the proper relations between the parts of the soul or the order stemming from reason that makes the soul a unified entity. In default of such order, mental unity eventually disintegrates, as in the case of the democratic soul in *Republic* IX (Cf. 423, 462, 432 A).

But not all unjust men are like the democratic man or the raving tyrant of *Republic* IX. One could be calculatedly wicked as Thrasymachus or be guided by 'cool self-love'.[21] The 'hedonic calculus' of the *Protagoras* could provide a sane alternative based on a long-term strategy, establishing order and priorities among one's desires and avoiding conflicts within one's soul. Plato had already shown the shortcomings of such 'hedonic calculus' in the *Protagoras*.[22] Although it does establish some order in the soul, its ruling principle is still desire as given content by each individual. What is missing from the hedonic calculus is the acknowledgment that the order of reason is prior to individual desires, and indeed to the individual himself. Protagoras' rational life strategy may avoid psychic disorder, at least to some extent, but it cannot circumvent the irreducible differences between the personal desires of the various members of society, except by recourse to some form of 'social contract'. Lacking any criterion on which to choose between opposing life plans or social structures, morality and social life must be founded on a compromise which, in Plato's eyes, is still basically irrational.

Ultimately, Plato thinks that plans of life guided by non-philosophical aims are also bound to be incoherent, as considered from a wider, non-individualistic point of view. Reason may be used calculatively, but only because it is more than that. What Plato advocates is not a maximization of pleasure, but a change of values. Some pleasures are objectively better than others, but even calculative reason has value. It is, after all, a reflection of normative reason on the lower levels of the soul. Thus, the many, who cannot fully attain this transvaluation of one's values, stand to gain from being made to lead moderate lives. Not only will they be freed from the evils arising from incontinence and recognize in retrospect that the change has been for the better,[23] but they will also participate in order and reason, albeit at a lower level, and benefit from their intrinsic value. Justice, for them too, will be desirable primarily for itself (although the many may not realize it and they may come to prefer it for its consequences).[24]

Submission to reason is always better, not only because of its consequences, but also in itself, although not if reason is conceived of as calculative, for then it is trivially desirable only because it is instrumental in achieving other goals, independent of it. Habituation develops the capacity of postponing gratifications, which is indispensable to the use of instrumental reason. Calculative reason is a consequence of habituation. Normative reason is always a consequence of understanding, i.e. of the capacity to give intrinsic reasons, whereas habituation is a matter of unexplained constant conjunctions. But understanding itself evolves from habituation. Calculative reason is a lower form of normative reason, not a different type of reason. It is harmony and teleology applied to extrinsic ends, not as considered in themselves. But habituation should also bring about a change in the choice of ends themselves, from ends independent of reason (and, to that extent, purely contingent) to ends dictated by reason (hence necessary in themselves). These are ends in which order and harmony are not subservient to other ends, but are constitutive of them, and are thus prior to the choosing individual. Rational ends are desirable in themselves, not because someone actually desires them.[25]

Human nature being what it is, not all are capable of this self-transcendence, of looking at themselves, as it were, from the outside, in a broader, synoptic perspective. But almost all are capable of seeing the point in the instrumental use of reason and of its application, at least in some measure, to their own ends. This, however, is not enough, as conflict may still arise, if not within the individual soul, then almost certainly between the ends of different individuals. In order to avoid such conflicts, or at least to restrict them to a minimum, habituation must also develop the right attitudes towards the cooperation and interdependence of which the fabric of the city is woven. In most citizens these attitudes will follow from a more or less unreasoned opinion about the nature of the city, possibly out of pragmatic considerations or out of habit and early education. And as all opinions, this opinion too is second best to knowledge, and it too, like Daedalus' statues in the *Meno*, can escape from the soul and must be fettered by the chains of reasoning.[26] Habituation will form the right character, but right character must be grounded in knowledge, if not in every individual (which is humanly impossible), then at least in the city as a whole.

In the ideal city of the *Republic*, this knowledge is impersonated in the philosopher-king. If complete understanding of the nature of justice is attainable, those who do attain it are uniquely qualified to rule the city in accordance with the aims of reason. All the others will live by opinion, formed from early childhood but grounded on absolute knowledge.

Plato is indeed paternalistic (if the term can be applied outside a liberal context). If there is someone who knows what is best – not best for you only, but best for all, hence for you too – he should be obeyed and he is entitled to impose reason 'from without'.

On the whole, we are ready to agree with Plato as long as we deal with children. Yet we do not think we are entitled to tell adults how they should manage their lives, unless they are patently incapable of caring for themselves – and even then we are not always sure when we have gone too far. But Plato thinks most people will never fully grow up morally. For him, moral growth is inseparable from intellectual growth. Most people will never attain full knowledge, and will thus never be able to see how their actions, attitudes and character fit in with the order of the city and of the universe. For Plato, most people will forever stay *in statu pupilari*.

Admittedly, there is some arbitrariness in our liberal outlook. Parents and other educators are given a limited time to do their job, until the child is sixteen or eighteen or twenty-one. After that, we let go, not necessarily because we have faith in the reason that the child has developed,[27] but rather because we think that, from a given point onwards, we no longer have the right to interfere with someone's pursuit of happiness as he sees it.

The many will thus be psychologically motivated to lead just and harmonious lives, according to right opinion. But opinion stems from persuasion, not from apprehension of the reason why.[28] It is intrinsically unstable; what makes it stay in the soul is external to its content. One may believe that justice pays because one has been brought up in an environment which encourages such beliefs, say by exposing people from an early age to stories and sermons to that effect, or by rewarding certain types of behaviour. The grip of such opinions on one's soul corresponds to the efficacy of the processes of socialization active in that society. These processes could just as well be geared – on purpose or by default – to achieving the opposite effect. That one lives through one's whole life in justice, like old Cephalus at the beginning of the *Republic*, guided by right opinion, is a fortunate accident. Cephalus himself admits that his wealth makes it easier for him to live justly.

In *Republic* X, Plato makes Er the Armenian come back from the underworld and report to us that the just will have their reward. Er saw the souls choosing their new lives before returning to earth. The first to choose was the soul of someone 'who had come from heaven, and had lived in his former life in a well-ordered city and had participated in virtue by habit and not by philosophy' (619 C6–D1). But Er also reported that this soul chose 'the mightiest of the tyrannies, from folly and greed . . . without making a thorough examination' (B8–9). That man was fortunate enough to have lived in a just city and to have had good habits and right opinions put into him. For his just life he was deservingly rewarded. He was also fortunate that he had never been faced with a temptation greater than his fortitude. But it could have happened. The unphilosophical just man lives in a perpetual moral danger. There is an uncertainty about the life of opinion which is not merely pragmatic. Even if the naively just does not falter to the end of his life, this is no more than 'moral luck', and he is still morally below the philosopher. Non-philosophical education is incomplete and imperfect. The philosopher leads a just life not by accident of birth or by orthodoxy but because he can see why his life is better; like Socrates in the *Phaedo*, he can give a *logos* of it. Were he offered the choice between his life and another, he would not have chosen otherwise. But he who lives by opinion cannot have such certainty. And this is also why the ideal city will degenerate and even the naively just will succumb to the foretaste of pleasure. Circumstances will change and people's opinions and characters, being extrinsically conditioned by them, will change too. And those who were model citizens in one environment may well end up, in different circumstances, as moral monsters. Plato had no misgivings about his ideal state,[29] but he had no illusions about the limits of education.

A note on the *Statesman*

In the *Statesman*,[30] Plato takes a closer look at the relations between the ruler and the ruled. If a philosopher-king could be found, that would be best. If there could be someone with absolute, synoptic knowledge, he would not need laws. He would be able to deal with each case on its own terms and merit. Statecraft is an art (*techne*); it has to do with particulars, although it is guided by rules. But rules can never take into account all the particular features of each case, and they can never fit all cases. Hence the importance given in Plato's analysis of the art of the ruler, in the *Statesman*, to the concept of the right moment (*kairos*). This concept stresses the element of particularity inherent in all political (and educational) decisions, which cannot be unequivocally determined by the rules. The philosophical ruler, if there were one, would be then perfectly justified in ignoring the law.[31]

The philosophical ruler would be the real statesman. He would have real knowledge, which his citizens would not have. Thus, there would be an important asymmetry in the relation between the philosophical statesman and his citizens. He would know what is best for them, while they would not. He would be more like a shepherd to his flock. Being essentially different from the citizens of his city, such a ruler would be a god, not a mortal (275 A).

Mortal kings will not be able to achieve absolute knowledge. Their rule will have to be based on laws, not to be infringed. The rule by law will be an attempt at imitating the rule of the philosophical statesman, and it will be evaluated by the measure in which it approximates it.

Thus, the *Statesman* does not supersede the *Republic*. The *Republic* sets up the ideal model against which all states are to be measured and which they strive to realize. To be a state is to imitate that model in some measure. The question is not whether the *Republic* was ever meant to be realized. Being an ideal, it sets standards. Like the ideas, it can be imitated but it cannot be reproduced.

The *Statesman* distinguishes between the model and its concrete imitations, good and bad. In passing from the model to the imitation, Plato stresses the imponderable particularity of each circumstance. But he is still diffident about the value of right opinion without knowledge. Only the true statesman will be able fully to take *kairos* into account. All others must 'keep strictly to the laws once they have been laid down and never transgress written enactments or ancestral costumes' (301 A), lest they claim falsely 'what only the truly wise ruler had a right to claim' (301 C).

Mere obedience to the law is opinion – at best, if the laws are good, right opinion. As such, it is fraught with all the evils and dangers of unreasoned belief. But, since at any given time most, possibly all, people will never be able to do more than that, obedience to the law is the best we can have.[32]

CHAPTER 12

An educator looks at literature and drama: *Republic* II–III, X

Emotion and cognition, in Plato's view, cannot be separated. All emotion has a cognitive component and all cognition implies an emotional attachment to its contents.[1] Reason, as we have already seen, develops from the irrational or the semi-rational. For Plato, the development of reason involves, firstly, the gradual clarification of the cognitive content of one's emotions and opinions. Socratic elenchus will purge false opinions and Platonic dialectic will seek reasons for those opinions which remain unrefuted. Concurrently, the development of reason involves the strengthening of the emotional attachment to the right objects, *viz.* to truth and being. Underlying all this process is the commitment to 'follow the *logos* to where it may lead us'.

Hence the twofold importance of literature in education, and especially in early education; literature shapes the character and inculcates opinions, or rather it shapes the character by inculcating opinions. The other arts, too, contribute to the formation of character. But music and dance influence more directly the emotional aspects of the soul, since their cognitive content is less obvious than that of the verbal arts. Painting and sculpture are, in this sense, halfway between literature and music.[2] Drama and literature, in particular, try to make opinions acceptable by aesthetic means. But aesthetic qualities as such are extrinsic to the content in question. They cannot serve as valid reasons for the opinions expressed or implied. They come instead of reasons. It is true that, for Plato, truth and beauty ultimately coincide. This is, for him, true art and true literature.[3] From that point of view we can see the shortcomings of literature as such. But, at the lower levels, where the cognitive content is blurred and not fully conscious, aesthetic qualities can have an appeal which is seldom dependent on the cognitive content. Aesthetic qualities can be pressed into service on either side of the moral case; the Great Inquisitor is no less convincing than Ophelia, nor is Baudelaire any less powerful than Petrarca.

It is not that literature and art cannot express insights into reality. But, in themselves, literature and art do not provide us with a criterion for distinguishing true insights from convincing but untrue pictures of the world. In Book X, Plato is concerned with the power of art to usurp reality. Giotto may have caught some essential aspect of the human and the divine. But how can we tell that his insight is any truer than the insights of Bosch or of De Chirico? The criteria of art are aesthetic, not epistemological, rhyme not reason.[4]

Literature is typically not argumentative. In so far as it is, it approximates philosophy. But not all literature in which ideas are discussed is philosophical. Antigone and Creon engage in discussions about law and morality, and Treplev in *The Seagull* makes speeches on the nature of art. But these serve primarily the overall delineation of the literary characters. Even when literature is agonistic or dialogical, its main interest remains the dramatic conflict between the characters, and only secondarily, if at all, does it aim at clarifying the issues involved and inquiring into the truth of the matter. To the extent that Sophocles and Chekhov expressed in those works opinions of their own about the matters discussed in them, these arise from the work as a whole rather than from an examination of the reasons.

Rather than search for the basic truth of the philosophical positions involved, the dramatist explores the consequences in action that follow from the characters' adopting certain positions. Shakespeare's interest is not in the examination of the philosophical assumptions of Renaissance free-thinking, but in the way Edmond's holding such ideas shapes his relations to the other characters.[5]

In the *Republic* Plato is interested in the educative influence of literature, and especially of tragedy. The educational aspect is never far from Plato's mind, but here it is foremost.[6] Literature cannot develop knowledge. But in developing opinion before knowledge can be developed, literature fulfils a role of capital importance. It educates by presenting concrete models for imitation. These models embody opinions about what is good and what is bad. The artist coaxes us into accepting those opinions not by showing us the reason why they are true, but by making them acceptable to the less cognitive parts of our soul.

One need not be Don Quixote to be influenced by literary works. How many were influenced by young Werther or by Lady Chatterley? We may not often take the painted couch for a real couch, but how often do we accept literary characters as real and tend to extrapolate from the novel or the play to real life, reacting emotionally and intellectually to literary characters as we would to real people?

Not surprisingly, it is the irrational character that is preferred in literary and dramatic presentation. The irrational character is dramatically more interesting. Literature depicts the emotions and caters to the emotional part of man. The more the writer is able to make us identify with irrational figures, the better we think of him. We praise Shakespeare for his characterization of Macbeth. But would we approve of someone who acted like Macbeth? We admire Odysseus and Achilles because of Homer's art; but the one was after all a deceiver, the other hot-tempered and greedy. So long as our admiration is confined to the *Iliad* and the *Odyssey*, there is little harm in it. But it may easily overflow into admiration of these traits of character also outside their literary context. Plato thinks that the pleasure we derive from the emotional reaction of others on the stage or in books may be, in the beginning, separated from the real-life behaviour of the reader or the spectator, but eventually it will influence real-life behaviour and we could sooner or later come to behave as those characters.

Rhetoric too appeals to the irrational parts of the soul. In it, too, aesthetic devices are used in order to achieve persuasion, along with other means. But rhetoric aims at influencing opinions and actions directly. Rhetoric is argumentative, or at least pseudo-argumentative. Literature, and drama especially, influence by setting concrete models for imitation, by making the particular characters who embody certain moral qualities seem to us admirable or loathsome, and by making them fare well or ill.

Plato is wary of the power of literature to make fictional characters and their implicit evaluation so plausible that we may come to accept a particular view of the world and of human action as a matter of course, because of the aesthetic and emotional influence of the work on us. Cinema and television can make violence acceptable and even admirable, through aesthetic means. Their influence, however, is not always restricted to the aesthetic domain. *Clockwork Orange* and *Rosemary's Baby* are two examples out of an ever-growing multitude.[7]

The highest object of imitation is God (383 C; cf. 613 A). This is, for Plato, almost tautological: 'God and all that is divine are in every way the best' (381 B4). God is the perfect embodiment of the good. He is the good considered as the object of imitation. The traditional gods are partial personifications of the good, so many objects of imitation.[8] As literature about the gods, mythology has thus a very serious educational function. The myth should be the highest form of literature, setting up the best models for imitation. But most of the myths about the gods, such as the story of the castration of Uranus by Cronos, and many others, can in no way serve this purpose.

In an obvious sense, these stories are not true. Surely, the myths about the gods are not to be taken literally. Nor are they simple allegories.[9] Myths have no simple referent. They signify by presenting a particular embodiment of an aspect of reality which cannot be empirically given, and hence cannot be literally described in particular terms. The truth of the myth, therefore, is not in the simple correspondence of its several statements to supposed states of affairs. It does not describe any particular state of affairs; it expresses in concrete terms a non-empirical truth. The truth of the myth is in its global correspondence to that non-empirical reality. The myth of the chariots of the souls in the *Phaedrus* is true, not because it describes things as they are but because it expresses, in terms of a particular image, a general truth about the nature of the soul.[10] The binding of Hera by Hephaestus or the hurling of Hephaestus from heaven by his father Zeus (378 D)[11] are false, not because they did not happen but because they implicitly commend certain types of action and traits of character which are morally unacceptable. And, conversely, the myth of reincarnation appropriated by Plato in *Meno* 81 is accepted because it will make us energetic and inquiring.[12]

Falsehood[13] as a property of statements, says Plato (382 Aff.), is of two types. A statement can be the expression of one's beliefs, but of course it need not be. One could tell the myth of the castration of Uranus believing it to be literally true or believing it to express a truth. in some way (e.g. by allegorizing it). This would be real falsehood, falsehood 'in one's soul'. Or one could tell the myth of the three metals (*Republic* 414 Dff.) or of the final judgment (*Gorgias* 523 Aff.), knowing that they do not literally describe things as they are but correspond in another way to some important aspect of reality, and lead to desirable ethical and social consequences.

In telling myths about the gods, we cannot claim to know that things are as we relate them. In fact, we know that they are not so in a simple sense. But we must try and make the falsehood as near the truth as possible. There are things we know about divinity; we know that it is not the cause of evil, that it is undeceptive and that it is simple and changeless (382 D). When we tell stories about the gods, we know what the truth is. We know that the events related did not take place and could not have taken place as told. But we also know that they express a moral injunction, and this moral injunction we can evaluate. If we are told about Cronos, that he castrated his father, this cannot be true, not because it did not happen – what would it be for it to have happened? – but because it sets up an unacceptable model for imitation.

Myths about the gods should then express the essential aspects of reality – unity, truth and goodness. Any myth that depicts divinity otherwise is false.[14] The full explanation of these attributes cannot come at this stage. Plato is taking us, too, through the stages of the education of the guardian. The progress from Book II to Book VII is itself a process of clarification, like the process the guardians are supposed to go through themselves. Only after arriving at the end of Book VII are we able to understand what has been done to us. It is in this sense that the idea of the good can be said to be already implicit in the early books of the *Republic*.

God or the gods are the ultimate object of imitation.[15] But the absolute simplicity and unchangeability of God cannot be directly imitated by men. Men need more immediate models. Ordinary people must have concrete models for imitation, for unphilosophical natures cannot imitate abstract structures. This is possible only if one has a complete understanding of the nature of virtue. Then, indeed, virtue is knowledge and if one has this perfect knowledge, one does not do evil knowingly. But, failing that, one must be content with concrete models – in some measure, at least.

These concrete models are provided by the myths about heroes. Heroes, being human but sons of gods, exemplify human virtues, but on a larger, idealized scale. The literal truth of the stories about heroes is also halfway between the myths of the gods and the stories about men. We cannot know the truth about the events related, but the factual content is in any case not to be taken too seriously. It matters relatively little whether or not King Solomon in fact ordered the baby to be halved, or whether Saint Francis actually preached to the birds. If these things were not so, it is fitting that they should have been so.

Myths about heroes offer immediate models for emulation. Thus, stories which make them unfit for such a role cannot be true as myth (and there is no point in inquiring into their historical truth). Heroes should not be depicted as displaying undesirable qualities of character. As idealizations of human virtue, they cannot be afraid of death, or be lacking in fortitude, or be prey to easy laughter or intemperance, or be fond of money and bribery. 'We shall not suffer our guardians to believe that Achilles . . . grandson of Zeus . . . was a lover of money and contemptuous of gods and men' (391 C). If Achilles is to be a model for the formation of character, this is necessarily false.[16]

As for stories about men (392 Aff.), nothing can be said at this stage, before the true nature of justice is clarified. Poets more often than not depict men who are unjust but happy, just but unhappy. That unjust men fared well, at least for a while, is a fact. Polus' example of the tyrant Archelaus, whom he thinks enviable,[17] is true in the simple sense that it states things as they happened. But these stories cannot be considered before considering the true nature of justice and finding out whether the just or the unjust are truly happy and successful, and how their presumed success is to be evaluated.

Myths about gods and heroes are in any case falsehoods. It is not their presumed factual content which makes them really true, but their ethical implications. In stories about men, however, there is always the straightforward telling of things that happened or are likely to happen.[18] And if the stories are faithful to the facts or to the probabilities, as in the case of Polus' description of Archelaus, in what sense then can they be said not to be true?

The answer can only be given after it has been shown that justice is naturally inherent in the human soul and in all human association, and that happiness is not subjective and empirical, but objectively evaluated according to criteria which are not purely psychological. This was done in the middle books of the *Republic*. The last book can then show that the artist goes wrong in that he represents the particular case and, in so doing, he distorts reality by shifting emphases, by evaluating things from a non-philosophical point of view, by describing man not as he truly is but as he appears to be.

The poet imitates the appearance of things, not their reality. Unjust men appear to fare well and the just do not seem to get their due. But the reality is the ideal human nature, complete with its non-utilitarian rewards. The poet claims that his representation captures the essence of man. Plato maintains that it represents only a doubly truncated imitation of reality. Edgar is not 'the thing itself'; he is at most a shadow of a shadow.

The individual man is only a partial, accidental representation of human nature. The artist, by selecting certain aspects and events of the life of an individual man, further restricts the representation of what man is. In particular, the poet does not take into account the non-empirical aspects of man. The tragedian is thus 'third from the truth' (597 E). He picks up certain aspects of the story of a man, which is in itself an imperfect representation of man's real life. From a moral point of view, it lacks especially the transcendental, non-utilitarian component.[19] The poet, then, has no real knowledge of those things he imitates. One can fairly easily agree not to go to Homer for medical advice. But Plato urges us also not to go to Strindberg for a *Weltanschauung*, persuasive as it may be.

'Imitative art imitates the actions of men, compelled or willing, thinking in every event that they have fared well or ill and in all these feeling sorrow or joy' (603 C4–8).[20] Now, man always has in himself contradictory impulses (603 D, cf. 435ff.), the one leading him to react to the situation at hand, the other to consider the further consequences of his actions and their wider context.

Literature, and especially drama, by appealing to the emotions, by making us commiserate with the immediate fate of the characters, encourages a myopic view of human affairs. The artist cannot be the true educator. Art distorts because it emphasizes. If one knows the real proportions, there is not much harm in this. But if not, the distortion may be dangerous. Here too, as in the *Protagoras*, Plato is prepared to go a long way with instrumental reason. But, as we saw above, instrumental reason is never enough.

Nevertheless, art is indispensable. Where reason is not yet developed, persuasion must be achieved by irrational means. Many of Plato's dialogues, such as the early ones, but also the *Phaedo*, try to do this. They are protreptic; they appeal to the non-philosophical soul, aiming to win it over to philosophy. Here the concrete story is ancillary to the argument, even if the argument proves to be only partially detachable from the concrete situation. In fact, that the argument is still partially dependent on the existential content[21] shows only the more forcefully that we still have to do with opinions. And the adequate insrument for dealing with opinions is literature, appealing as it does to the irrational or semi-rational aspects of man. The primary aim of Plato's Socratic dialogue is to show the way to philosophy. The Socratic dialogue is philosophy only in the sense that the way to philosophy is itself philosophy. But that way can be long and tortuous, as shown by many of the earlier dialogues.

Yet, Plato denies that literature, and art in general, can be autonomous. Art depicts the individual and the particular, and these are for Plato essentially dependent and derivative. Therefore, serious literature must be guided by philosophy. Literature as an educative tool – and it cannot avoid being so – should set man's actions and his reactions to their consequences in a wider perspective, which takes into account also the ideal component in human life. It must consider human events from the supra-personal vantage point of a synoptic knowledge. The real artist must be, too, 'the spectator of all eternity'.

Aristotle, on the contrary, thought that literature, and especially tragedy, can give us real insights into man's nature. We recognize ourselves in the tragic hero and by going vicariously through his experiences, we understand the human predicament common to all of us. But, for Aristotle, the criteria for the evaluation of traits of character and of the actions issuing from them are immanent.[22] The particular situation has in it all that is needed, or all that can be had, for a decision, right or wrong. This is part of what is meant by saying that Aristotle's forms are in things, not apart from them.

Not so for Plato. Plato maintains that the criteria for the evaluation of actions and traits of character are not to be found only by examining the particular action and its consequences. Tragedy focuses on particular actions and situations and on the agent's subjective evaluation of them as causing him joy or sorrow. Most tragedy is false in Plato's eyes because it accepts the evaluation of the events of the plot on their own terms. But Plato cannot accept that a plot, as a causal series of events, can be complete in itself, with beginning, middle and end, without reference to standards of evaluation which are not given in the plot itself, but stem from considerations independent of, and prior to, the causal series.

The *Phaedo* is the Platonic counterpart of a tragedy. It is the representation of Socrates' actions on his last day, and of his evaluation of them and their consequences in terms of joy and sorrow. Young

Phaedo's view of the situation contrasts sharply with Socrates'. Phaedo grieves over Socrates' death, but Socrates measures success and failure by the fate of the argument, not by his own. Again, the final myth of the *Phaedo* provides a different perspective on the events, which cannot be extracted from the events themselves. Socrates does not consider his own death the end of the matter and it is not by it that he judges himself happy or unhappy.[23]

Likewise the final myth of the *Republic* put human life within a wider perspective, from a non-empirical point of view. 'It must be assumed[24] about the just man that, though he live in poverty, in disease or any other seeming evil, these things will in the end work out well for him in his life or even[25] after death' (613 Aff.). The myth is a temporal representation of a non-temporal reality. It is the image of normative reason as instrumental reason, as a means to an end, i.e. it expresses a non-temporal teleological order as extended in time.

It is thus that myth is for Plato the highest form of literature. It is the closest literature can come to a direct imitation of the ideas, still without being philosophy. The myth is not the story of the events it seems to relate, but a concrete representation of ideal reality, as far as such a representation is possible.

The concluding myth of the *Republic* is a falsehood, like all myths. But, in the sense explained above, it is true, whereas Glaucon's myth of the magical ring of Gyges[26] is false. Both myths present hypothetical states of affairs in order to explore aspects of the moral situation which cannot be given in direct experience. But Socrates' myth directs our interest away from purely psychological motivation, while Glaucon's stresses it all the more. And, as always with Plato, it is the moral consequences that count; if we believe in what Er is said to have reported, we shall always follow justice and wisdom, and we shall fare well, although not necessarily by utilitarian criteria and perspectives.

Notes

Chapter 1 Introduction

Good general introductions to Plato's philosophy are G.M.A. Grube, *Plato's Thought*, London, Methuen, 1935, New York, Beacon Press, 1958; A. Koyré, *Discovering Plato*, tr. L.C. Rosenfield, New York, Columbia University Press, 1945; D. Ross, *Plato's Theory of Ideas*, Oxford, Clarendon Press, 1951; J.E. Raven, *Plato's Thought in the Making*, Cambridge University Press, 1965; G.C. Field, *The Philosophy of Plato*, 2nd ed., Oxford University Press, 1969. Among the numerous more detailed expositions, see A.E. Taylor, *Plato, The Man and His Work*, London, University Paperbacks, 1929; P.Friedlander, *Plato*, 3 vols, London, Routledge & Kegan Paul, 1958–69; I.M. Crombie, *An Examination of Plato's Doctrines*, 2 vols, London, Routledge & Kegan Paul, 1962–3; J.C.B. Gosling, *Plato*, London, Routledge & Kegan Paul, 1973; W.K.C. Guthrie, *A History of Greek Philosophy*, vols IV–V, Cambridge University Press, 1975–8; N. Tigerstedt, *Interpreting Plato*, Stockholm, Studies in the History of Literature, vol. 17, 1977; N.P. White, *Plato on Knowledge and Reality*, Indianapolis, Hackett, 1978. See also T. Irwin, *Plato's Moral Theory: The Early and Middle Dialogues*, Oxford, Clarendon Press, 1979.

An indispensable bibliographical tool is H. Cherniss, 'Plato 1950–1957', *Lustrum*, vol. 4, 1959, vol. 5, 1960, including also items anterior to 1950; continued in L. Brisson, 'Plato 1958–1975', *Lustrum*, vol. 20, 1977, and in R.D. McKirahan Jr, *Plato and Socrates: A Comprehensive Bibliography 1958–1973*, New York, Garland, 1978. See also the extensive bibliographies in Friedlander, *op. cit.*, and Guthrie, *op. cit.*

On Plato's views on education, see J. Stenzel, *Platon der Erzieher*, Leipzig, F. Meiner, 1928; R.L. Nettleship, *The Theory of Education in Plato's Republic*, Oxford University Press, 1935; W. Jaeger, *Paideia: The Ideals of Greek Culture*, tr. G. Highet, Oxford University Press, vols II–III, 1939–45; H.I. Marrou, *A History of Education in Antiquity*, tr. G. Lamb, New York, Sheed & Ward, 1956, Ch. VI; G.M.A. Grube, *Plato's Thought*, London, Methuen, 1935, Ch. VII. See also R. Barrow, *Plato, Utilitarianism and Education,* London, Routledge & Kegan Paul, 1975, and *Plato and Education,* London, Routledge & Kegan Paul, 1976. For a short appreciation, see R.S. Peters, 'Was Plato nearly right about education?', *Didaskalos*, vol. 5, 1975, pp. 3–16.

1 On the other hand, there is no reason to assume that just because Xenophon's Socrates is the less interesting he must be the more historical. Xenophon, like Aristophanes and Aristotle, each in his own way, may help direct our attention to aspects of Socrates' biography, personality and doctrines. But it is Plato's Socrates that we are finally left with. For Xenophon's Socrates, cf. L. Strauss, *Xenophon's Socrates*, Ithaca and London, Cornell University Press, 1972.

2 On the 'Socratic problem', see Guthrie, *A History of Greek Philosophy*, vol. III, Cambridge University Press, 1969, Ch. XII.

3 On the order and chronology of Plato's dialogues, see Ross, *Plato's Theory of Ideas*, Oxford, Clarendon Press, pp. 1ff.; Guthrie, *A History of Greek Philosophy*, vol. IV, Cambridge University Press, 1975, pp. 41ff.; and cf. also H. Thesleff, *A Study in the Styles of Plato*, Helsinki, Finnish Academy, Acta Philosophica Fennica, vol. 20, 1967, and especially his *Studies in Platonic Chronology*, Helsinki, Societas Scientiarum Fennica, Commentaria Humanorum Litterarum, vol. 70, with exhaustive comparative tables and extensive bibliography.

4 On Plato's method of hypothesis, see pp. 89ff. in this book.

5 On the unifying function of Plato's theory of ideas, see H. Cherniss, 'The philosophical economy of the theory of ideas', *American Journal of Philology*, vol. 57, 1936, pp. 445–56, repr. in G. Vlastos (ed.), *Plato: A Collection of Critical Essays*, vol. I, London, Macmillan, 1971, pp. 16–27.

Chapter 2 The background and the challenge: sophistic education

On the sophists, see W.K.C. Guthrie, *A History of Greek Philosophy*, vol. III, part 1, Cambridge University Press, 1969 (also published separately as *The Sophists*); E.A. Havelock, *The Liberal Temper in Greek Politics*, New Haven and London, Yale University Press, 1957; G.B. Kerferd, *The Sophistic Movement*, Cambridge University Press, 1981; H. Sidgwick, 'The sophists', *Journal of Philology*, vol. 93, 1872, pp. 288–307, vol. 94, 1873, pp. 66–80. For good summaries of sophistic education, see W. Jaeger, *Paideia*, tr. G. Highet, Oxford University Press, 1939, vol. I, pp. 286ff.; and H.I. Marrou, *A History of Education in Antiquity*, tr. G. Lamb, New York, Sheed & Ward, 1956, Chs IV–V.

1 *Protagoras*, 310 Af.

2 'Excellence' is, in most cases, less misleading than 'virtue' as a translation of *arete*, although I shall be using the latter word, too, when more appropriate. The Greek concept 'could be qualified as excellence in a particular accomplishment or art', and originally implied also valour and nobility, although the connotation of social class recedes with time. See W.K.C.

Guthrie, *A History of Greek Philosophy*, vol. III, Cambridge University Press, 1969, Ch. X.

3 Cf. Protagoras, fr. 3 Diels-Kranz: 'Instruction (*didskalia*) requires talent and exercise' and 'One should start learning from youth'. Education cannot be left only to the family and the political environment. It needs natural endowment, but this must be developed by purposeful training.

4 On the traditional excellences, cf. A.W.H. Adkins, *Merit and Responsibility*, Oxford, Clarendon Press, 1960, Ch. III; H. North, *Sophrosyne: Self-knowledge and Self-restraint in Greek Literature*, Ithaca, NY, Cornell University Press, 1966. Pericles' funeral speech in Thucydides II 35–46 gives the fifth-century BC Athenian ideal.

5 On the relation of the speculative and the practical in Protagoras and Gorgias, see below.

6 Protagoras, fr. 1 DK.

7 Relativism itself was not Protagoras' innovation. Xenophanes, towards the end of the sixth century BC, had already based his criticisms of Homeric theology on the relativity of men's conceptions of the deity. But he, like his predecessors, assumed an objective truth distinct from the appearances.

8 Fr. 6a, cf. A 20. See also A 19. If p is a proposition and x and y are two different persons, then 'p for x' and 'not-p for y' are obviously not contradictory.

9 Fr. 6b.

10 A 5 = Plato, *Protagoras* 318 D.

11 Cf. *Theaetetus* 167 Bff., and pp. 63–4 in this book.

12 These questions will better be discussed in the chapter on Plato's *Protagoras*, p. 21ff. in this book.

13 Protagoras postulates justice and reverence as two distinct principles. Plato, following Socrates, thought that knowledge is a sufficient motive for action. For him, therefore, the recognition of the validity of the principle of justice should by itself lead to action according to it, and thus justice and reverence could be integrated into a single principle.

14 Plato elaborates on the view of Protagoras in the dialogues *Protagoras* and *Theaetetus*. See below, Chs 4 and 8.

15 Gorgias refers to his *Helen* as 'a trifle'; cf. fr. 11 end.

16 Cf. George Kennedy, *The Art of Persuasion in Greece*, London and New Haven, Princeton University Press, 1963, pp. 62–3.

17 Fr. 3. Cf. Guthrie, *A History of Greek Philosophy*, vol. III, Cambridge University Press, 1969, pp. 192ff.

18 Cf. Augustine, *The Teacher*, tr. J.M. Colleran, New York, Newman Press, 1978, Ch. 10, section 33.

19 Cf. Ch. 5 in this book.

20 *Memorabilia* IV 4, 6.

21 On Hippias, see Marrou, *A History of Education in Antiquity*, tr. G. Lamb, New York, Sheed & Ward, 1956, pp. 54–6; R. Brumbaugh and

N.M. Lawrence, *Philosophical Themes in Modern Education*, Boston, Houghton Mifflin, 1973, pp. 25–35; Guthrie, *A History of Greek Philosophy*, vol. III, Cambridge University Press, 1969, pp. 280–5.
22 Fr. 44. This same point is developed further by Critias, fr. 25. Seeing that the laws were being flouted in secret, some 'wise and acute man devised the mortals' fear of the gods, who see all and hear all' and do not countenance injustice.
23 Frs 60, 62.
24 Aristotle, *Politics*, III 9. 1280 b8ff., II 8. 1267 b22ff.
25 As Marrou, *A History of Education in Antiquity*, tr. G. Lamb, New York, Sheed & Ward, 1956, pp. 89ff., points out.
26 On Plato's views on rhetoric, art and literature, cf. Chs 5 and 12 in this book.
27 *Antidosis* 266.
28 *Antidosis* 271.
29 *Antidosis* 274.
30 *Antidosis* 277.
31 *Antidosis* 252. For the similarity to *Gorgias* 456–7, and in general for the question of the parallels between Isocrates and Plato, see E.R. Dodds, *Plato: Gorgias*, Oxford, Clarendon Press, 1959, *ad loc.*, p. 212, and Guthrie, *A History of Greek Philosophy*, vol. IV, Cambridge University Press, 1975, pp. 308ff.
32 For a general assessment of Isocrates and his impact on Western education, see Marrou, *A History of Education in Antiquity*, tr. G. Lamb, New York, Sheed & Ward, 1956, pp. 79ff.

Chapter 3   Socrates on the unity of the person

On Socrates, see A.H. Chroust, *Socrates, Man and Myth*, London, Routledge & Kegan Paul, 1957; W.K.C. Guthrie, *A History of Greek Philosophy*, vol. III, part 2, Cambridge University Press, 1969 (also published separately as *Socrates*); M.J. O'Brien, *The Socratic Paradoxes and the Greek Mind*, Chapel Hill, University of North Carolina Press, 1967; N. Gulley, *The Philosophy of Socrates*, London, Routledge & Kegan Paul, 1968; G. Santas, *Socrates*, London, Routledge & Kegan Paul, 1979; R.E. Allen, 'The Socratic paradox', *Journal of History of Ideas*, vol. 21, 1960, pp. 256–65; G. Vlastos (ed.), *The Philosophy of Socrates*, Garden City, NJ, Anchor Books, 1971.

1 *Apology* 38 A5.
2 Aristotle, *Protrepticus*, fr. 11 Walzer.
3 Cf. Aristophanes, *Clouds* 225ff.; Plato, *Phaedo* 96 A6.
4 See *Phaedo* 58 B, where much is made of the word in that context. Cf. L. Brandwood, *A Word Index to Plato*, Leeds, W.S. Maney, 1976, *s.v.* therein.

5 The 'binding of opinions by the fetters of reasoning' in *Meno* 98 A8 is probably Platonic, but it is hardly more than a metaphorical description of Socrates' demands in the earlier dialogues.

6 Cf. *Crito* 47 D4, *Protagoras* 312, and J. Burnet, 'The Socratic doctrine of the soul', *Essays and Addresses*, London, Chatto & Windus, 1929, pp. 126–62.

7 Aristotle thought more highly of tradition and common sense, but even for him, these were only starting points.

8 Cf. *Charmides* 188 D, 193 D, *Gorgias* 482 B.

9 Cf., e.g., *Charmides* 159 A10, *Meno* 83 D2, 85 B8ff.

10 Cf. *Gorgias* 466 E4–7. Socrates is sometimes also prepared, rather facetiously, to ascribe an opinion to his interlocutor if it follows from his other avowed opinions. Cf., e.g., *Gorgias* 466 E4.

11 Cf. my *Plato's Method of Hypothesis*, unpublished PhD thesis, University of Cambridge, 1973, Ch. 3.

12 Cf. *Gorgias* 504, *Republic* 609. At least so far, the common ground of the Socratic and the Platonic views of the soul is not much different from, e.g., the view presented in C. Frankenstein, *Roots of the Ego*, Baltimore, MD, Williams & Wilkins, 1966, Ch. 6, esp. p. 66. But the similarities between Socrates (or Plato) and analytic psychology should not be exaggerated.

13 The archaic view of moral responsibility is notoriously complex. Cf., e.g., *Odyssey* I 33ff.: evil comes to men *spheisin atasthaliesin*, through their own folly, but Orestes' killing of Aegisthus is preordained. Cf. W.H. Adkins, *Merit and Responsibility*, Oxford, Clarendon Press, 1960, pp. 50ff., with G. Vlastos' strictures in *Plato's Universe*, Seattle, University of Washington Press, 1975, pp. 13ff. At any rate, the innovation is not so much in the concept of moral responsibility as such as in the attribution of moral responsibility to a *unified personality*. But, of course, this is not to say that there is in archaic thought no characterization; Achilles is irascible and Odysseus is cunning. What is lacking is the recognition of character as the *locus* of moral responsibility.

14 Fr. 119 DK.

15 But the Greek concept of *ethos* does not include the element of will, which is implied in the English 'character'. Indeed, whether or not the Greeks had any concept comparable to our *will*, with its voluntaristic implications, such a concept did not play any significant philosophical role in classical times.

16 See further B. Snell, *The Discovery of Mind*, tr. T.G. Rosenmeyer, New York, Harper & Row, 1960, Ch. 8.

17 T. Irwin, *Plato's Moral Theory*, Oxford, Clarendon Press, 1977, p. 91, takes the value of self-examination to lie in the importance of the correct beliefs about morals which are arrived at in that process. But, intrinsic considerations apart, the passages he adduces do not support his contention. I should take *Apology* 38 A to be squarely against this view. *Gorgias* 457 E refers indeed to reaching right opinion 'about whatever the dis-

cussion happens to be'; however, this has to do with the general case of knowledge (or right opinion) being good in itself, not with correct moral beliefs. *Charmides* 157A and *Gorgias* 500 C are either inconclusive or prove the contrary of what Irwin needs.

18 See, e.g., *Apology* 19 Df., where Socrates contrasts himself to Gorgias, Prodicus, Hippias and a lesser sophist, and disclaims having any knowledge or teaching anything. See also *Charmides* 165 B, *Protagoras* 348 C, 361 D, *Gorgias* 506 A.

19 The god does to Socrates what Socrates does to others; he presents him with a paradox which arouses Socrates to inquiry.

20 *Apology* 22 D.

21 Cf. Irwin, *Plato's Moral Theory*, Oxford, Clarendon Press, 1977, pp. 63–4. But I cannot see that 'a Socratic definition will not analyse the concept inarticulatedly grasped by the ordinary speaker'. It is true that the concept is modified in the course of the analysis and parts of it are rejected altogether. None the less, the starting point is still the more or less confused grasp of the educated man in the street.

22 Aristotle, *Sophistic Refutations* 183 b7. Cf. also Plato, *Theaetetus* 150 C and *Republic* 337 A.

23 On the logical aspects of the Socratic elenchus, see R. Robinson, *Plato's Earlier Dialectic*, Oxford, Clarendon Press, 1953, Chs 2 and 3, repr. in G. Vlastos, *The Philosophy of Socrates*, New York, Anchor Books, 1971, pp. 78–109. The emotional aspects of elenchus have not been stressed nearly enough. See, however, Adkins, *Merit and Responsibility*, Oxford, Clarendon Press, 1960, pp. 34, 266ff., who also calls attention to the Homeric meaning of *elenchos* as shame at one's failure in word or deed. See further my 'Three aspects of Plato's philosophy of learning and of instruction', *Paideia*, vol. 5, 1976, pp. 50–62.

24 *Meno* 89 C.

25 Or for his followers. Cf. Protagoras. A19 DK.

26 Cf. R.K. Sprague, *Plato's Use of Fallacy*, London, Routledge & Kegan Paul, 1962. But Socrates seems not to be totally innocent of *philoneikia*, or contentiousness, even in Plato's eyes. Cf., e.g., *Gorgias* 515 B.

27 The joke in Aristophanes, *Clouds* 137, falls flat if *Theaetetus* 149ff. is wholly Plato's invention. For the controversy on the historicity of Socrates' *maieutike*, see W.K.C. Guthrie, *A History of Greek Philosophy*, vol. III, Cambridge University Press, 1969, pp. 397 n. 1 and 444–5 n. 3. See further pp. 60–1 in this book.

28 For irony as understatement, see Aristotle, *Nicomachean Ethics* 1108 a23.

29 Cf. G. Vlastos, 'The paradox of Socrates', in *The Philosophy of Socrates*, Garden City, NJ, Anchor Books, 1971, pp. 16–17.

Chapter 4 Education, Teaching and Training: *Protagoras*

On the *Protagoras*, see W.K.C. Guthrie, *Plato: Protagoras and Meno*, introduction and translation, Harmondsworth, Penguin, 1956; *Protagoras*, Benjamin Jowett's translation, extensively revised by Martin Ostwald, edited with an introduction by Gregory Vlastos, Indianapolis, Bobbs-Merrill, 1956; C.C.W. Taylor, *Plato: Protagoras*, tr. with notes, Oxford, Clarendon Press, 1976. See further G.M.A. Grube, 'The structural unity of the *Protagoras*', *Classical Quarterly*, vol. 27, 1933, pp. 203–7; W.K.C. Guthrie, *A History of Greek Philosophy*, vol. IV, Cambridge University Press, 1975, Ch. V; A. Koyré, *Discovering Plato*, tr. L.C. Rosenfield, New York, Columbia University Press, 1945; G. Vlastos, 'The unity of virtues in the *Protagoras*', *Review of Metaphysics*, vol. 25, 1972, pp. 415–58, repr. with additions and corrections in his *Platonic Studies*, Princeton University Press, 1977, pp. 221–65.

1 On the date of the *Protagoras*, see Guthrie, *A History of Greek Philosophy*, vol. IV, Cambridge University Press, 1975, pp. 213–14.

2 *Kallion*, comparative of *kalos*, fine, noble in an aesthetic as well as in a moral sense, in opposition to *aischron*, base, shameful. The argument about courage, at 359f., is conducted in terms of *aischron* and *kalon*.

3 On the significance of the opening scene with Hippocrates, see further A. Koyré, *Discovering Plato*, tr. L.C. Rosenfield, New York, Columbia University Press, 1945, p. 19.

4 Hippocrates' excitation parallels that of the unnamed friend in the frame story (cf. 309 D3ff. and 310 B7ff.). He could use the 'hedonic calculus' discussed in the dialogue.

5 The question of the possibility of a purely formal education (here represented by rhetoric) is not raised in this dialogue, as Protagoras himself did not seem to have held such a thesis. But the *Gorgias* is wholly dedicated to attacking this position. Here I differ somewhat from C.C.W. Taylor's interpretation of this passage (in his *Plato: Protagoras*, Oxford, Clarendon Press, 1976).

6 This point is made even more clearly in the *Gorgias*.

7 Cf. pp. 9–10 in this book.

8 Note that these are (with the understandable omission of stereometry) the same sciences that make up the first part of Plato's higher curriculum. But Hippias did not integrate them within a theory of knowledge and of education, as Plato did. In much the same way, Prodicus' linguistic analysis resembles Socrates' quest for definitions. But, as far as we know, Prodicus did not use his verbal distinctions to examine moral questions, nor did he attach to them any ethical significance, even when dealing with matters of morality, as in his 'Heracles at the crossroads' (paraphrased by Xenophon, *Memorabilia* II 1 21–34).

9 Cf. 321 D and contrast *Republic* 326 C–328 A. See G.M.A. Grube, 'The

structural unity of the *Protagoras*', *Classical Quarterly*, vol. 27, 1933, pp. 203–4.

10 On reverence and justice, see pp. 7–8 in this book.

11 More recently by G. Vlastos, 'The unity of virtues in the *Protagoras*', *Review of Metaphysics*, vol. 25, 1972, pp. 415–58, and C.C.W. Taylor, *Plato: Protagoras*, Oxford, Clarendon Press, 1976.

12 For an analysis of Socratic induction (*epagoge*), see R. Robinson, *Plato's Earlier Dialectic*, Oxford, Clarendon Press, 1966, pp. 46–8.

13 I thus disagree with Vlastos' interpretation of the argument in his otherwise excellent introduction to the *Protagoras* (Indianapolis, Bobbs-Merrill, 1956), pp. xxi–xxxvi.

14 The Greeks traditionally conceived of the law as also prescribing appropriate behaviour and educating the character, and not only, as in the liberal tradition, as restricting the scope of permissible actions. For the dissenting view, cf. pp. 10–11 in this book.

15 Cf. Ch. 12 in this book.

16 See further C.C.W. Taylor, *Plato: Protagoras*, Oxford, Clarendon Press, 1976.

17 This is precisely where Meno goes wrong, at *Meno* 96.

18 Cf. also C.C.W. Taylor, *Plato: Protagoras*, Oxford, Clarendon Press, 1976, pp. 134f. Protagoras does not indeed espouse here any version of evaluative relativism, 'i.e., the doctrine that the standards by which things are judged good or bad vary in different circumstances . . . and there is no second-order criterion by which it is possible to judge any standard more correct than any other'. But his examples are all facts of nature (as Taylor notes), and evaluative relativism would be out of place in this context. But if nature and society are discontinuous – and this is in fact Protagoras' position – then the question of evaluative relativism makes sense again.

The lack of objective standards of judgment is made clear again in the short exchange at 334 D, immediately following the passage we are dealing with. When Socrates complains of Protagoras' long speeches, the latter asks whether he should make his answers 'as long as necessary', and proceeds to offer two possibilities: 'As long as *I* think necessary, or *you*?' He does not raise a third possibility; as long as the subject-matter itself demands (cf. *Phaedrus* 264ff.). Guthrie's translation at 334 D6–7 is misleading. What Protagoras says is: 'Am I to make them shorter than necessary?'

19 The obvious parallel is J. Bentham, *Principles of Morals and Legislation*, Ch. IV.

20 That Socrates' argument is dialectical, from his opponent's premises, has been maintained, among others, by Grube, 'The structural unity of the *Protagoras*', *Classical Quarterly*, vol. 27, 1933, pp. 203–7, and by F.M. Cornford, *Cambridge Ancient History*, Cambridge University Press, 1953, vol. VI, p. 313. Vlastos, in his Introduction to the translation of

the *Protagoras* (Indianapolis, Bobbs-Merrill, 1956), p. xl n.50, takes the opposite view.

21 Protagoras would have had little difficulty in recognizing his own position in the following paragraph:

> we are dealing with an area that isn't a matter of proof or consensus. It is a matter of experience. So, if a child says that he likes something, it does not seem appropriate for an older person to say, 'You shouldn't like that.'. . . If these things have grown out of a child's experience, they are consistent with his life. When we ask him to deny his own life, we are in effect asking him to be a hypocrite . . . . Every individual is entitled to the views that he has and to the values that he holds, especially where these have been examined and affirmed. As teachers, then, we need to be clear that we cannot dictate to children what their values should be since we cannot also dictate what their environments should be and what experiences they will have . . . . In areas involving aspirations, purposes, attitudes, interests, beliefs, etc., we may raise questions, but we cannot 'lay down the law' about what a child's values should be. By definition and by social right then, values are personal things. (Louis E. Rath, Merril Harwin and Sidney Simon, *Values and Teaching: Working with Values in the Classroom*, Columbus, Ohio, Charles F. Merrill, 1966, pp. 36–7)

But, living in a non-pluralistic society, Protagoras would probably insist that in order 'to become more purposeful, more enthusiastic, more positive, and more aware of what is worth striving for' (*ibid.*, p. 12) one must be fully integrated into one's society.

22 On sophistic education as an expression of public opinion, cf. *Republic* 492.

23 Nevertheless, Plato recognizes the role of pleasure, or of the gratification of desires, in education. See *Republic* 582ff., *Philebus* 53 C, *Laws* 732 D–733 D.

24 See 353 E5 and C.C.W. Taylor's note in his *Plato: Protagoras*, Oxford, Clarendon Press, 1976, pp. 175–6. There is no need to translate, with Guthrie and with Ostwald, 'So the only reason why these pleasures seem to you to be evil is, *we suggest*, etc.' Socrates could very well be taken, with Jowett and with Croiset, to be saying: 'Don't you think, *as Protagoras and I maintain*, etc.', provided this is understood as his position *in this argument*. It would not be the only time Socrates argues on his interlocutor's premises. Cf. also G. Vlastos' review of T. Irwin's *Plato's Moral Theory*, in the *Times Literary Supplement*, 24 February 1979.

25 Cf. Theaetetus 178 Cff., and pp. 66–7 in this book.

Chapter 5 The impossibility of neutrality: *Gorgias*

On the *Gorgias*, see E.R. Dodds, *Plato: Gorgias*, text, introduction and notes, Oxford, Clarendon Press, 1959; W. Hamilton, *Plato: Gorgias*, introduction and translation, Harmondsworth, Penguin, 1960; T. Irwin, *Plato: Gorgias*, introduction, translation and notes, Oxford, Clarendon Press, 1979; W.K.C. Guthrie, *A History of Greek Philosophy*, vol. IV, Cambridge University Press, 1975, pp. 284–312.

1 *Gorgias* 456 C6ff., *Meno* 95 C.
2 For a discussion of some contemporary versions of this problem, see my 'Truth, neutrality and the philosophy teacher', in M. Lipman and A.M. Sharp (eds), *Growing Up with Philosophy*, Philadelphia, Temple University Press, 1978, pp. 392–404, and bibliography there, pp. 402–3 n. 1. I cannot take here into full account T. Irwin's commentary on the *Gorgias* (Oxford, Clarendon Press, 1979), but two general points should be made:

   (a) Plato does not reject the view that no one does wrong willingly. See, e.g., *Timaeus* 86 E, and my 'Reason and passion in the Platonic soul', *Dionysius*, vol. 2, 1978, pp. 35–48.
   (b) Irwin (*Plato: Gorgias*, Oxford, Clarendon Press, 1979) underestimates the importance of Socrates' dialectical method. The Socratic procedure is always to argue from the premises of the opponent and from within the opponent's own conceptual framework. The *Protagoras* is a case in point, often misunderstood.

3 Cf., e.g., *Gorgias* 461 Bff., *Phaedrus* 259–74.
4 Cf., e.g., J. Dewey, *How We Think*, Boston, Heath, 1933, Ch. VI.
5 See, for example, the spate of books on programmed instruction in almost all subjects and on behaviour modification in the classroom, which has only recently subsided.
6 Max Black quotes the following passage from an interview of Professor L.F. Fieser: 'It's not my business to deal with political or moral questions. That is a very involved thing. Just because I played a role in the technological development of napalm doesn't mean [sic] I'm any more qualified to comment on the moral aspects of it' ('Scientific neutrality', *Encounter*, vol. 51, 1978, p. 62).
7 In the *Hippias Minor*, Socrates argues that 'the good man is thus no other than he who errs and of his own will does shameful and unjust acts, *if there is such a man*' (376 B4–6). But, as the stressed words suggest, Socrates is arguing from premises that he does not necessarily accept, and he is in fact producing a *reductio ad absurdum*.
8 Cf. Dodds, *Plato: Gorgias*, Oxford, Clarendon Press, 1959, p. 15.
9 On Gorgias' epistemological nihilism, see pp. 8–9 in this book.
10 Socrates distinguishes, with Gorgias' approval, between *memathekenai*,

'being in a state of having learned', and *pepisteukenai*, 'being in a state of having been persuaded' (454 C7ff.). He uses the Greek perfect and refers to *states*, not to the *processes* that produce such states. Cf. *Meno* 81 C7, D1, where the distinction is even more important, since the process implied is recollection, not learning in the ordinary sense, yet the final state is the same as in our passage.

11 Cf. *Gorgias* 454 Df. with I. Scheffler, *Conditions of Knowledge*, Chicago, Scott, Foresman & Co., 1965, pp. 12–13. Of course, Scheffler's use of 'knowledge' and 'truth' is wider than Plato's use of *episteme* and *aletheia*. For Plato's distinction between knowledge (*episteme*) and opinion or belief (*pistis*, *doxa*), see *Meno* 97ff., *Republic* 511 and *Theaetetus* 201 A–B, where the present passage is reformulated in somewhat different terms (also in *Statesman* 304 C10).

12 For other types of rhetoric, cf. *Phaedrus* 261.

13 On the related problem of the 'weakness of the will', see, e.g., G. Mortimer (ed.), *Weakness of Will*, London, Macmillan, 1971.

14 Cf. *Phaedrus* 271 D.

15 Cf. *Gorgias* 495. I have further developed this point in my 'Three aspects of Plato's philosophy of learning and instruction', *Paideia*, vol. 5, 1976, p. 58.

16 *Republic* 515 Cff.

17 Cf. also Thrasymachus' disavowal at *Republic* 349 A9–10.

18 *Helen* 14. Gorgias is not necessarily implying a dualism of soul and body.

19 Cf., e.g., R. Schmidt, 'Leadership', *Encyclopedia of the Social Sciences*, New York, Macmillan, 1933, vol. IX, p. 282: 'Strictly speaking, the relation of leadership arises only where a group follows an individual from free choice and not under command or coercion and, secondly, not in response to blind drives but on positive and more or less rational grounds' (quoted by A.S. Tannenbaum, 'Leadership: sociological aspects', *International Encyclopedia of the Social Sciences*, New York, Macmillan, 1968, vol. IX, p. 102).

20 Cf. Tannenbaum, 'Leadership: sociological aspects', *International Encyclopedia of the Social Sciences*, vol. IX, New York, Macmillan, 1968, p. 101, with *Gorgias* 452 E.

21 Cf. pp. 37–8 in this book. I cannot concur with Irwin's (*Plato: Gorgias*, Oxford, Clarendon Press, 1979) generous remark to 474 C, that Polus sees, or at least does not deny, that we may have reason to act morally even against our own interests'.

22 On the argument at 467 C5–468 E5, see p. 39 in this book.

23 Cf. Dodds, *Plato: Gorgias*, Oxford, Clarendon Press, 1959, p. 251. But *Protagoras* 333 D9, which he quotes as a parallel is a question put to Protagoras, not a statement of Socrates.

24 Cf. G. Vlastos, 'Was Polus refuted?', *American Journal of Philology*, vol. 88, 1967, pp. 455–6 n. 3.

25 Vlastos, 'Was Polus refuted?', *American Journal of Philology*, vol. 88, 1967, pp. 454–60, argues that Polus need not have conceded defeat, for Socrates is basing his induction at 474 D4ff. on cases such as bodies, colours, sounds, etc., which are called 'noble' or 'beautiful' (*kala*) because they are useful or because they delight those who see or hear or contemplate them. In doing evil and suffering evil, however, the answer to the question ' "Which is the more painful *for those who observe* or contemplate the two events?" ... is, at best, indeterminate' (p. 458, Vlastos' italics).

It seems to me that Vlastos misses the point of Socrates' argument. In the case of bodies, colours and sounds, Socrates clearly has in mind a dyadic relation, in which are involved the object and the beholder (or the hearer), and the object 'is useful for some particular purpose' or 'produces delight in the beholder in beholding it' (*en to theoreisthai khairein poiei tous theorountas*). In this case, a triadic relation (which is what Vlastos needs) is impossible. Similarly, in the case of doing evil, only the act of doing evil and the agent are envisaged (although a triadic relation is possible, as Vlastos' construction requires, but is unwarranted by the analogy). Socrates' question is whether the act of doing evil is more painful or more harmful *to the agent* than its alternative, just as he asked (e.g. in the *Laches*) if exercise in armoured combat is advantageous because it develops courage *in him who is engaged in such exercise*, or if a law is better than another because it is more useful (to the organization of society or to the education of the citizens) *for those whose law it is* – not for a third, disinterested observer.

26 *Republic* 338ff. and 343 Aff. Cf. pp. 105 and 110–11 in this book.

27 T. Hobbes, *Leviathan*, Ch. xi.

28 But see reservations, *Republic* 583–5, *Philebus* 31–2, 51ff., *Timaeus* 64ff.

29 Cf. D. Hume, *A Treatise of Human Nature*, vol. II, book iii, part 3, quoted at p. 73 of this book. Hume speaks of the *will*, but the Greeks apparently did not have such a concept of will, as a purely motive, non-deliberative psychic faculty.

30 Plato couldn't make this point here. A consideration of intrinsic values would have to fall back on a fully developed metaphysics, which is not available to him in this dialogue.

31 The reasoning is parallel to that of the 'hedonic calculus' in the *Protagoras*.

32 See, e.g., I. Berlin, 'Two concepts of liberty', *Four Essays on Liberty*, Oxford, Clarendon Press, 1958.

33 Cf. Ch. 9.

34 Cf. Dodds' note to this passage in his *Plato: Gorgias*, Oxford, Clarendon Press, 1959. pp. 218–19.

35 Against Irwin (*Plato: Gorgias*, Oxford, Clarendon Press, 1979) on 505 B–C, I do not think Plato recognized good-independent desires. Cf., e.g.,

Meno 77 B7, 78 B2; all desires are good-dependent but one may be misguided about their relative order and subordination.

36 A. Kenny, 'Mental health in Plato's *Republic*', *The Anatomy of the Soul*, New York, Barnes & Noble, 1973, p. 2, thinks 'mental health' in the *Gorgias* is only an allegory, which gives way to theory building in the *Republic*. See also J.P. Anton, 'Dialectic and health in Plato's *Gorgias*: presuppositions and implications', *Ancient Philosophy*, vol. 1, 1980, pp. 49–60.

Chapter 6   Sophistic or Socratic? *Euthydemus*

On the *Euthydemus*, see R.K. Sprague, *Plato: Euthydemus*, translation and notes, New York, Bobbs-Merrill, 1965; R.K. Sprague, *Plato's Use of Fallacy: A Study of the Euthydemus and Some Other Dialogues*, London Routledge & Kegan Paul, 1962; W.K.C. Guthrie, *A History of Greek Philosophy*, vol. IV, Cambridge University Press, 1975, pp. 266–83.

1 Polymathy: cf. *Euthydemus* 271 C6 with *Hippias Major* 285 Bff.; linguistic analysis: *Euthydemus* 277 E; peripateticism: cf. *Euthydemus* 273 A3 with *Protagoras* 314 E4; instant *arete*: cf. *Euthydemus* 273 D8–9 with *Protagoras* 318 A5ff.; disregard for other types of knowledge: cf. *Euthydemus* 273 D1–4 with *Protagoras* 318 D5ff.; denial of contradiction: cf. *Euthydemus* 285 Dff. and p. 6 in this book; arguing both sides: see, e.g., *Euthydemus* 275 Dff., and for Protagoras, cf. *ibid* in this book. Cf. also Socrates' introduction of Clinias to the two brothers, at 275 A–B, with his introduction of Hippocrates to Protagoras, at *Protagoras* 316 B–C.

2 For Isocrates, cf. pp. 11–12 in this book.

3 Cf. *Protagoras* 319 A.

4 J.F. Herbart, *The Science of Education*, book II, ch. 1, section 2, tr. H.M. and E. Felkin, Boston, D.C. Heath & Co., 1902, pp. 126–7.

5 R.K. Sprague is right in observing, in her annotated translation of the *Euthydemus, ad* 275 AB (New York, Bobbs-Merrill, 1965), that 'they [sc. Euthydemus and Dionysodorus] merely desire to obtain a respondent for a demonstration of their eristic tricks'. But she should not have compared the present passage to *Parmenides* 137 B and *Sophist* 217 D. Parmenides and the Eleatic Guest are no sophists, and Theaetetus, the respondent in the latter dialogue, is certainly no fool.

6 Cf. *Protagoras* 313 Aff., and p. 22 in this book.

7 Cf. *Theaetetus* 150 E–151 B.

8 The second horn of the dilemma is developed as a variation on this theme: see 276 D.

9 The second part of the *Parmenides* is perhaps the best example of an exhaustive presentation of a field of discourse. But this is achieved there at the cost of extreme formalism.

10 Cf. also *Meno* 81 B9–10, *Cratylus* 329 E, *Republic* 477–8. See further G. Prauss, *Platon und der logische Eleatismus*, Berlin, W. de Gruyter, 1966, p. 125. Problems notoriously arise under further analysis, as Plato shows in the *Sophist*, but these are beyond the scope of the present book.

11 A similar doctrine appears in the *Cratylus*. Cf. the previous note and pp. 84ff. in this book.

12 One has to presume a sulky silence on the part of Dionysodorus after Socrates' words at E2–3.

13 Contrast with Socrates' insistence on the coherence and the unity of the personality in Ch. 3 of this book.

14 This was later to be an accepted Stoic doctrine. Cf., e.g., Diogenes Laertius VII 101–5.

15 *Meno* 81 D1–4 already enunciates briefly the Platonic counterpart of *Euthydemus* 294 A2–3: all nature is akin and if only one knows one single thing, nothing prevents one from knowing all things. And cf. p. 99 in this book.

16 *Ktesis*. The Greek is ambiguous.

17 Another limited success is the geometry lesson on the *Meno* itself.

18 Cf. *Republic* 601 C–602 A and Aristotle, *Nicomachean Ethics* 1098 b32.

19 For a discussion of some aspects of the philosopher-king in this passage and in other dialogues, see R.K. Sprague, *Plato's Philosopher King: A Study of the Theoretical Background*, Columbia, SC, University of South Carolina Press, 1976.

20 'To give a share' translates 292 B8 *metadidonai*; cf. 273 D8 *paradounai*, 'to hand down', on p. 44 of this book.

21 On education as initiation, cf. R.S. Peters, 'Education as initiation', in R.D. Archambault (ed.), *Philosophical Analysis and Education*, London, Routledge & Kegan Paul, 1965, pp. 78–111.

22 Cf. *Charmides* 169ff.

23 It is difficult not to suppose that the reference is to Isocrates, although other identifications have been proposed. Crito himself, of course, fits the description of the anonymous observer quite well.

24 I cannot follow Leo Strauss' analysis, leading to the conclusion that 'in the *Euthydemus* Socrates takes the side of the brothers against Ktesippus and Kriton'. See his 'On the *Euthydemus*', *Interpretation*, vol. 1, 1970, pp. 1–20.

Chapter 7 The concept of learning: *Meno*

On the *Meno* and on recollection, see R.S. Bluck, *Plato's Meno*, introduction, text and commentary, Cambridge University Press, 1961; W.K.C. Guthrie (tr.), *Plato: Protagoras and Meno*, Harmondsworth, Penguin, 1965; M. Brown (ed.), *Plato's Meno*, Indianapolis, Hackett, 1971 (Guthrie's translation with a selection of articles); J.A. Klein, *A Commentary on Plato's Meno*, Chapel Hill, University of North Carolina Press, 1965; R.G. Hoerber, 'Plato's "Meno" ', *Phronesis*, vol. 5, 1960, pp. 78–102; R.E. Allen, '*Anamnesis* in Plato's *Meno* and *Phaedo*', *Review of Metaphysics*, vol. 13, 1959, pp. 165–74; G. Vlastos, '*Anamnesis* in the *Meno*', *Dialogue*, vol. 4, 1965, pp. 143–67; J.L. Ackrill, '*Anamnesis* in the *Phaedo*', in E.N. Lee, A.P.D. Mourelatos and R.M. Rorty (eds), *Exegesis and Argument*, Assen, Van Gorcum, pp. 177–95.

For a modern re-interpretation of the *Meno's* dilemma, see H.G. Petrie, *The Dilemma of Enquiry and Learning*, Chicago and London, University of Chicago Press, 1981.

1 Cf. Plato's pun at 71 C8: *Ou panu eimi mnemon, o Menon* ('I am rather weak at mnemonics, Meno').

2 Cf. p. 9 in this book.

3 Cf., e.g., J.R. Martin, 'On the relation of "Knowing that" to "Knowing how" ', in B. Othanel Smith and R.H. Ennis (eds), *Language and Concepts in Education*, Chicago, Rand MacNally & Co., 1961, p. 62.

4 B. Phillips, 'The significance of Meno's paradox', *Classical Weekly*, vol. 42, 1948–9, pp. 87–91, points out the difference between Meno's and Socrates' versions of the *aporia*. He was followed by J. Moline, 'Meno's paradox?', *Phronesis*, vol. 14, 1965, pp. 153–61.

5 Cf. *Euthydemus* 275 D, p. 45 in this book. But Socrates' question is not quite the sophist's paradox. Plato, as usual, appropriates a sophistic argument for his own ends.

6 What Socrates asks the boy at 82 B9–10 is, literally: 'Do you know a square area that it is like this' (*gignoskeis tetragonon khorion hoti toiouton estin*)? Note that *know* is here a triadic relation.

7 Socrates says: 'these [lines] here through the middle' (82 C2–3). These must be the diagonals, not the medians. A lozenge too has four equal sides and two equal medians. But four equal sides and two equal diagonals unambiguously define a square. And the solution asked for is already there from the beginning. (Cf. 84 A1, 'if you do not want to calculate, show which one.')

8 Cf. 83 B7: 'No, by Zeus!'

9 The necessity of such conceptual revolution will be elaborated on in the *Phaedo* and especially in the simile of the Cave in *Republic* VII, where Plato stresses the pain involved in losing one's familiar conceptual world. But the assumptions there are not necessarily to be read into the *Meno*. See also Ch. 8 in this book.

10 *p* is the proposition, p is the object or state of affairs. Plato prefers to speak of knowledge of the fact instead of knowledge of the proposition.

11 Cf. p. 29 in this book.

12 Cf. Aristotle's middle term as the reason or account of the extremes, in *Posterior Analytics* B 8.

13 *Hen ge ti eidos tauton hapasai ekhousi* di'ho *eisin aretai.* Cf. *Euthyphro*
6 D with the instrumental dative instead of *dia.*

14 Meno takes Socrates' point reluctantly at 73 D1, substituting the non-
causative *kata* for Socrates' *dia*: 'if you do seek a certain one over all'
(*epei hen ge ti zeteis kata panton*). The contrast between *dia* and *kata* in
this passage is too marked to be trivial. Bluck's examples (*Plato's Meno*,
Cambridge University Press, 1961) of *kata* used by Socrates at 76 A4–5
and 88 E5 are irrelevant to the relation between the one *eidos* and the
many things that have its name. The question of the relation of the particulars to the idea is further inquired into in the *Phaedo*, esp. 75 Cff.,
there too within the context of recollection. See further A. Nehamas,
'Plato on the imperfection of the sensible world', *American Philosophical
Quarterly*, vol. 12, 1975, pp. 105–17.

15 On the epistemological status of Platonic myths, cf. Ch. 12 in this
book.

16 One should note how this ambiguity is carefully guarded by Plato, e.g. in
the precise formulation of the myth of *anamnesis*. As Klein, *A Commentary on Plato's Meno*, Chapel Hill, University of North Carolina Press,
1965, p. 179, pointed out, Plato does not say that the soul *learned* in a
previous life what she now knows, but uses the perfect tense throughout:
'she was in a state of having learned' (81 C7, D2, 86 A2, 8; also
heorakuia, 81 C6).

17 Bluck, *Plato's Meno*, Cambridge University Press, 1961, p. 414.

Chapter 8   Recollection revisited: *Theaetetus*

On the *Theaetetus*, see F.M. Cornford, *Plato's Theory of Knowledge*,
London, Routledge & Kegan Paul, 1935; J. McDowell, *Plato: Theaetetus*,
translation with notes, Oxford, Clarendon Press, 1973; W.G. Runciman,
Plato's Later Epistemology, Cambridge University Press, 1962; W.K.C.
Guthrie, *A History of Greek Philosophy*, vol. V, Cambridge University
Press, 1978, pp. 61–122. See also G. Fine, 'Knowledge and logos in the
Theaetetus', *Philosophical Review*, vol. 88, 1979, pp. 366–97.

1 The *Theaetetus* clearly belongs to the group of dialogues later than the
Republic, although it does have some characteristics of the earlier
dialogues (e.g. it is aporetic). It is discussed here in order to stress its
thematic relation to the *Meno*.

2 As, e.g., Guthrie, *A History of Greek Philosophy*, vol. V, Cambridge
University Press, 1978, p. 120, thinks.

3 Cf. *Sophist* 248.

4 See pp. 19–20 in this book.

5 Plato's use of *anamimnesthai* four times in this dialogue can hardly be

accidental. Cf. 142 C4 and 143 A2 in the frame-story, 209 C8 at the end, and 166 E2, on which see below.

6 Cf., e.g., *Meno, Phaedo, Phaedrus, Republic*.

7 Cornford, *Plato's Theory of Knowledge*, London, Routledge & Kegan Paul, p. 83.

8 Cf. *Phaedo* 81 A.

9 *Tithentes*, a technical term for assuming a hypothesis.

10 *Parmenides* 142 Dff.

11 Cf. 156 B; Cornford, *Plato's Theory of Knowledge*, London, Routledge & Kegan Paul, p. 30.

12 Here Plato drops the terminology of perception, but the basic contention remains unchanged; things are for each one what they seem to him (or to them, if the subject is taken collectively).

13 Cf. pp. 84ff. in this book.

14 Cf. *ephaptesthai*, 154 B1, 190 C6, D9.

15 Cf. *Parmenides* 163 B7–166 C5.

16 Cf. McDowell's detailed analysis (*Plato: Theaetetus*, Oxford, Clarendon Press, 1973) with Guthrie, *A History of Greek Philosophy*, vol. V, Cambridge University Press, 1978, pp. 75ff.

17 Cf. *Euthydemus* 287 A, and p. 47 in this book.

18 Cf. p. 7 in this book.

19 On the argument, see Guthrie, *A History of Greek Philosophy*, vol. V, Cambridge University Press. 1978, p. 87. Against S. Tigner, The "exquisite" argument at *Tht.* 171', *Mnemosyne*, ser. 4, vol. 24, 1971, p. 369, see E.N. Lee, ' "Hoist with his own petard": ironic and comic elements in Plato's critique of Protagoras (*Tht.* 161–171)', in E.N. Lee, A.P.D. Mourelatos and R.M. Rorty (eds), *Exegesis and Argument*, Assen, Van Gorcum, 1973, pp. 245–9. Cf. especially Lee's analysis of Protagoras' inability to extricate himself from the use of relativizers, 'for him', 'for me'; Protagoras could not really say anything to us, only report his states of mind – which was what the claims of the later sceptics were reduced to; cf. Sextus Empiricus, *Outlines of Pyrrhonism*, I (vii) 15.

20 This is a sort of Aristotelean argument 'from the sciences' (*ex epistemon*). The fact that there is a science or expertise can best be explained on the hypothesis that there is objective truth (e.g. ideas). Conversely, if Protagoras' relativism holds, science and expertise are impossible. The argument is not so much that each science must have an object of its own, as that true knowledge or science (*episteme*) must refer to an objective reality.

21 Cf. *Republic* 359 A, and pp. 101–2 in this book.

22 Cf. especially 175 B9, suggesting the escape from the cave, and C2 on the consideration of justice itself and injustice, what each of them is, and in what they differ from each other and from anything else' – with which cf. 201ff.

23 *Doxa* refers both to the act (judgment) and to its product (opinion).

24 What is 'acceptance' or 'assent'? Plato does not go explicitly into this question. But see on Socrates, Ch. 3 in this book:

(a) there must be a minimal emotional attachment to the position expressed (this will be important in the *Symposium* and in the descent to the cave);

(b) it must be minimally consistent with at least some of the other propositions held by the respondent (Plato does not believe one can be totally insensitive to contradiction, see p. 33 in this book).

25 Not 'potential'. 'Potential' implies the possibility of development: 'latent' implies only its being non-apparent. Aristotle picks up the distinction between possessing knowledge and actually exercising it (cf. *Physics* IX4. 255 b2 and *On the Soul* II 1), but reinterprets it within his own conceptual network. F.A. Lewis, 'Foul play in Plato's aviary', E.N. Lee, A.D.P. Mourelatos and R.M. Rorty, *Exegesis and Argument*, Assen, Van Gorcum, 1973, following J.L. Ackrill, suggests 'dispositional'/'actualized'. But 'dispositional' is too weak, quasi-behaviouristic, and unnecessarily brings up the question of counterfactuals.

26 Cf. *Phaedo* 103ff.

27 So, rightly Lewis, 'Foul play in Plato's aviary', *Exegesis and Argument*, pp. 267–8.

28 Cf. 198 B4 *paradidonai* with *Euthydemus* 273 D8, p. 44 in this book.

29 Cf. *Meno* 85 C10ff.: 'If he is asked these same things repeatedly and in many ways, he will come to know them as well as anyone else.'

30 The conditions of these interconnexions are examined in the *Parmenides* and in the *Sophist*.

31 204 A2 *sunarmotte*; 201 E2, B3 *sunkeimene*. Contrast 203 C6 *suntethenton*.

32 Cf. also *Timaeus* 30 C2ff. with *Parmenides* 142 D6ff.

33 The overall scheme of the hypotheses in the *Theaetetus* is as in Figure N.1, p. 138, below.

Chapter 9 The perfectibility of the individual: *Phaedrus* and *Symposium*

On the *Phaedrus* and the *Symposium*, see R. Hackforth, *Plato's Phaedrus*, introduction, translation and commentary, Cambridge University Press, 1952; W.K.C. Guthrie, *A History of Greek Philosophy*, vol. IV, Cambridge University Press, 1975, pp. 365–433; R.G. Bury, *The Symposium of Plato*, edited with introduction, critical notes and commentary, 2nd edition, Cambridge, W. Heffer & Sons Ltd, 1969 (first published 1909); W. Hamilton, *Plato: the Symposium*, introduction and translation, Harmondsworth, Penguin, 1951; S. Rosen, *The Symposium of Plato*, New

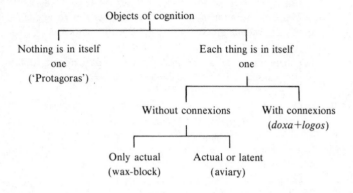

Figure N.1 The overall scheme of the hypotheses in the Theaetetus.

Haven, Yale University Press, 1968; T.M. Robinson, *Plato's Psychology*, Toronto, University of Toronto Press, 1970; L. Robin, *La théorie platonicienne de l'amour*, Paris, J. Vrin, 1933; T. Gould, *Platonic Love*, Routledge & Kegan Paul, 1963; F.M. Cornford, 'The doctrine of Eros in Plato's *Symposium*' (1938), *The Unwritten Philosophy and Other Essays*, Cambridge University Press, 1950, pp. 68–80; L.A. Kosman, 'Platonic love', in W.H. Werkmeister (ed.), *Facets of Plato's Philosophy, Phronesis*, Supplement 2, 1976, pp. 53–69; G. Vlastos, 'The individual as object of love in Plato', *Platonic Studies*, Princeton University Press, 1977, pp. 3–42; D. Levy, 'The definition of love in Plato's *Symposium*', *Journal of History of Ideas*, vol. 49, 1979, pp. 285–91.

1 David Hume, *A Treatise of Human Nature*, vol. II, book iii, part 3, London, Dent (Everyman's Library), 1911, p. 125.
2 Lacking, as all Greeks, a concept of will pure and simple, Plato usually speaks of desires (*epithumiai*), which are roughly emotion (or passion) plus will, i.e. a non-cognitive feeling involving a drive (positive or negative). In this context, I take 'emotion' and 'passion' to be equivalent. That, contrary to common opinion, desires do have a cognitive aspect is a central part of Plato's argument. Cf. also *Republic* 580 D7ff., on each part of the soul having its own three parts.
3 On *eros*, see especially G.M.A. Grube, *Plato's Thought*, London, Methuen, 1935, Ch. III; G. Vlastos, 'The individual as object of love in Plato', *Platonic Studies*, Princeton University Press, 1977, pp. 3–42.
4 It is a moot point whether the speech is actually by Lysias or a parody by Plato himself. In the present context the matter is of small consequence. On the authorship of the speech, see G. Kennedy, *The Art of Persuasion in Greece*, Princeton University Press, 1963.

5 On Greek homosexuality, see K.J. Dover, *Greek Homosexuality*, London, Duckworth, 1978. On Plato's view, see also the judicious chapter by Grube, *Plato's Thought*, London, Methuen, 1935, Ch. III.

6 Cf. 236 B1 *hupotithestai*, 'it was laid down'.

7 Two sorts of what? Plato does not specify, although the context would lead us to complete 'of desires'. But, at this stage, the possibility remains that the other sort is not simply a desire in the usual sense. See below.

8 On the non-committal translation of *doxa*, see Hackforth, *Plato's Phaedrus*, Cambridge University Press, 1952, pp. 41–2.

9 See pp. 26ff. in this book, on the *Protagoras*.

10 On the function of myths in Plato, see pp. 114ff. in this book.

11 For Plato, the ideas are the real *phusis*. Cf. his use of the word in, e.g., *Republic* 298 A1.

12 The same proof recurs in *Republic* 608 Dff. and is referred to in *Laws* 895 E10ff. In the *Phaedo*, Plato has a somewhat different proof.

13 *Pasa psukhe*. See n. 15 below.

14 *Aeikineton*. There is a variant *autokineton*, 'self-moving', which was accepted by Robin (*La théorie platonicienne de l'amour*, Paris, Vrin, 1933), but does not fit the argument. For a defence of the traditional reading and the logic of the argument, see T.M. Robinson, 'The argument for immortality in the *Phaedrus*', in J.P. Anton and G.L. Kustas (eds), *Essays in Ancient Greek Philosophy*, Albany, State University of New York Press, 1971, pp. 345–53.

15 *Pasa psukhe* could mean either. The article, variously inserted in the manuscript tradition at 246 B6, does not help.

16 Moreover, Plato refers to the presumed learning process of the discarnate soul in very ambiguous terms: she 'is in a state of having learned' (*memathekuia*, *Meno* 81 D1) or 'in a state of having seen' (*heorakuia*, *Meno* 81 C6, cf. *tetheatai*, *Phaedrus* 249 E4–5). Hackforth, *Plato's Phaedrus*, Cambridge University Press, 1952, p. 65 n. 1, must be wrong in maintaining that Plato thought he could prove individual immortality.

17 *Symposium* 178 A6–180 B8.

18 On the *Lysis*, see also D. Bolotin, *Plato's Dialogue on Friendship*, Ithaca and London, Cornell University Press, 1975; R.G. Hoerber, 'Plato's *Lysis*', *Phronesis*, vol. 4, 1959, pp. 15–28.

19 A broken statue is deficient because it lacks a piece (which is complementarily deficient in the same way). The completion of the statue is a matter of simple addition. A bad statue is imperfect because it is not up to standard.

20 On the concepts of completion, as developed in the *Lysis*, and perfection, as developed in the *Symposium*, cf. Bolotin, *Plato's Dialogue on Friendship*, Ithaca and London, Cornell University Press, 1975, Appendix, summarizing the controversy between von Arnim and Pohlenz. The metaphysical counterpart of the Aristophanic split is what Aristotle

called the 'separation' of Plato's ideas; the true nature of things is not immanent in them.

21 Cf. *Republic* X 611 B–D, and my 'Reason and passion in the Platonic soul', *Dionysius*, vol. 2, 1978, pp. 35–50.

22 Usually translated as 'friendship', as between the citizens of the same state, and occasionally as 'love', as between husband and wife. Cf. also next note.

23 Aristotle's classical treatment of *philia* is in the *Nicomachean Ethics*, books VIII–IX. On *philia* being for the sake of one's *philos*, cf., eg., 1155 b31, 1156 b9–10, 1159 a9; on *philia* based on merit, cf. book VIII, Chapter 11; on reciprocity, cf. 1161 b28, 1163 b6, 1170 b6, etc. (commercial contracts too belong to the context of *philia*); the *philos* another self, cf. 1166 a31; objective good as what is loved (*philein*) in one's *philos*, cf. 1157 b4, 1158 b4.

24 Aristotle's prime mover is, of course, the object of *eros*, not of *philia*. Otherwise, *eros* is an excess of *philia* (*Nicomachean Ethics* IX 10. 1171 a11, cf. 1158 a11), i.e. an imbalance of what should primarily be a reciprocal relation.

25 Cf. I. Kant, *The Doctrine of Virtue*, Part II of *The Metaphysics of Morals*, section 39 Note, tr. M.J. Gregor, New York, Evanston and London, Harper & Row, 1964, pp. 133–4.

26 E.g. John 3.16: 'For God so loved (*egapesen*) the world, that he gave his only begotten Son.' Anders Nygren, *Agape and Eros*, tr. P.S. Watson. London, SPCK, 1953, is one-sided but still indispensable for an understanding of *agape*. See also T. Gould, *Platonic Love*, London, Routledge & Kegan Paul, 1963.

27 *Euthydemus* 283 C3ff.

28 I should not have belaboured this point, were it not for G. Vlastos' influential paper, 'The individual as object of love in Plato', *Platonic Studies*, Princeton University Press, 1977, pp. 3–42.

29 Cf. *Phaedo* 81 A1: philosophy is a 'practice for death' (*melete tanathou*).

30 *Timaeus* 86 Eff.

31 Such as the 'genetic lottery', represented in the final myth of the *Republic* by the casting of the lots. Cf. Adam's note to *Republic* 618 A2, quoting Plotinus II ii 15, in *The Republic of Plato*, Cambridge University Press, 1902, 2nd ed. 1963, repr. 1965.

Chapter 10 Method and truth: *Republic* V–VII

On the *Republic*, see J. Adam, *The Republic of Plato*, introduction, text and notes, Cambridge University Press, 2 vols, 2nd ed., 1963; A.D. Lindsay, *Plato's Republic*, introduction and translation, London, Dent, 1935; F.M. Cornford, *The Republic of Plato*, introduction, translation and notes, Oxford,

Clarendon Press, 1942; R.C. Cross and A.D. Woozley, *Plato's Republic: A Philosophical Commentary*, London, Macmillan, 1964; J.E. Raven, *Plato's Thought in the Making*, Cambridge University Press, 1965; A. Sesonske (ed.), *Plato's Republic: Interpretation and Criticism*, Belmont, California, Wadsworth, 1966; N. White, *A Companion to Plato's Republic*, Oxford, Blackwell, 1979; J. Annas, *An Introduction to Plato's Republic*, Oxford, Clarendon Press, 1981.

1 Although, as the *Theaetetus* will clarify, the object of knowledge is not put together of elements. Cf. pp. 71f. in this book.

2 *Meno* 97 A10ff.

3 Not unlike some modern versions of 'epistemological anarchism', e.g. P.K. Feyerabend, *Against Method*, London, Verso, 1975.

4 Or 'the equals themselves'. I do not think any appreciable difference has been shown to exist between *auta ta isa* at 74 C1 and *auto to ison* at 74 C4–5, E7, 9.

5 Cf. *Phaedo* 71ff. See A. Nehamas, 'Plato on the imperfection of the sensible world', *American Philosophical Quarterly*, vol. 12, 1975, pp. 105–7.

6 See pp. 66f. in this book.

7 As maintained by Isocrates (p. 11 in this book) and by Callicles at *Gorgias* 485.

8 Cf. *Meno* 97 C6ff., 98 B2–5.

9 *Oukoun episteme men epi toi onti pephuke, gnonai hos esti to on*. Note the abrupt transition from the two-place to the three-place predicate formulation. J. Gosling, '*Doxa* and *dunamis* in Plato's *Republic*', *Phronesis*, vol. 13, 1968, pp. 124f., thinks the second clause is a gloss on the first, by Plato himself. But this is surely strange; the characterization of knowledge as triadic recurs emphatically twice, once at 477 B10–11, before the discussion of the difference between opinion and knowledge, and again at 478 A6, during that discussion. As we shall see, the argument in fact depends on the understanding of knowledge (and opinion) as a three-place predicate. Taking the second part of the statement, *to on gnonai hos esti* (or *hos ekhei*) as an essential part of the definition of knowledge goes together with taking *eph' ho* and *ho apergazetai* ('about what' and 'what it accomplishes') as two independent criteria of cognition and not as redundant or implying each other, as Gosling has it. The conclusion that opinion is of (or about, *epi*) something different from knowledge will not follow unless it is granted that a difference between *dunameis* is jointly defined by a difference between their respective objects and between 'what they accomplish'.

10 Cf. *Parmenides* 132 B3–C11, where Plato explicitly rejects the alternative: if ideas are thoughts (*noemata*), what are they thoughts of?

11 *Republic* V 476 E5–8; cf. *Meno* 97 C9–10. But in both passages Plato studiously avoids the triadic formulation, for dialectical reasons.

12 Cf. pp. 46f., 134 n. 6 in this book
13 For the undertanding of 'being' as incomplete for 'being *F*', see *Republic* 478 D5–479 B10.
14 There is no convenient English word for *doxazon*. The irrelevant connotations of 'believer' are too strong.
15 In this passage, Plato does not deal explicitly with error as misrecognition, but this is presupposed in the analogy of opinion to dreaming.
16 It follows that the beautiful itself is beautiful in a different way from that in which the sensible beautiful things are beautiful. The literature on the so-called self-predication of the Platonic ideas is immense. Some of the classical articles on this subject are reprinted in R.E. Allen, *Studies in Plato's Metaphysics*, London, Routledge & Kegan Paul, 1965. See further G. Vlastos, *Platonic Studies*, Princeton University Press, 1973, and A. Nehamas, 'Self-predication and Plato's theory of forms', *American Philosophical Quarterly*, vol. 16, 1979, pp. 93–103. For what I take to be Plato's solution, cf. my 'Il *Parmenide* di Platone: Prolegomini ad una re-interpretazione', in F. Romano (ed.), *Momenti e Problemi di Storia del Platonismo, Symbolon*, vol. 1, Università di Catania, 1984, pp. 9–36.
17 Cf. *Republic* 479 A, *Phaedo* 74 B7–10, *Symposium* 211 A1–5.
18 Cf. *Phaedo* 103 B7, 92 D9, *Parmenides* 130 E6.
19 The philosopher's apprehension of the sensible world is distinct from the opinion of the other dwellers of the cave in that it is accompanied by the awareness of its not being knowledge. That this last type of cognition is not mentioned in the Line shows, firstly, that Plato's conception of the relation between knowledge and opinion is more complex than is normally assumed, and, secondly, that the Line is not intended to be an exhaustive classification of the modes of cognition.
20 *Eikos logos* or *eikos muthos*. Cf., e.g., *Timaeus* 30 B7, 59 C6, 68 D2.
21 I shall be using the capitalized words 'Sun', 'Line' and 'Cave' to refer to the similes, and the lower-case 'sun', 'line' and 'cave' to designate the objets themselves.
22 Cf. 516 C7–D2.
23 Cf. *Timaeus* 67 B, 80 A.
24 Cf. E. Heitsch, 'Die nicht-philosophische *aletheia*', *Hermes*, vol. 90, 1962, pp. 24–39, following M. Heidegger, *Platos Lehre von der Wahrheit*, Bern, A. Francke, 1947.
25 I believe the method of hypothesis to be essentially the same throughout the dialogues from the *Meno* onwards. I have discussed it at length in my *Plato's Method of Hypothesis in the Middle Dialogues*, unpublished PhD thesis, Cambridge University, 1974, and more summarily in 'Hypothetical method and rationality in Plato', *Kant-Studien*, vol. 66, 1975, pp. 157–62, from where the next few paragraphs were adapted.

26 See R. Robinson, *Plato's Earlier Dialectic*, 2nd ed., Oxford University Press, 1953, p. 94.

27 Cf. *Gorgias* 499 E, 503 E–504 A, *Timaeus* 30 Cf., and *Phaedrus* 265 D–E. On intelligibility and teleology in Plato, cf. my 'An image of perfection: the good and the rational in Plato's *Timaeus*', forthcoming.

28 Robinson, *Plato's Earlier Dialectic*, 2nd ed. Oxford University Press, 1953, p. 146.

29 Cf. *Meno* 98 B2–5: 'However, that right opinion is something different from knowledge, this I do not believe to imagine, but if I say I know any-thing – and there are few things I say I know – this I lay down as one of the things I know.'

30 As did Kant and most modern philosophers after him. Plato would not have accepted Scheffler's weakening of his second condition of knowledge and especially his notion of 'adequate evidence' as 'good reasons' varying with the nature of the subject (cf. his *Conditions of Knowledge*, Glenville, Ill., Scott, Foreman & Co., 1965, Ch. 3, esp. pp. 56–9). Reasons which, in Plato's terms, are themselves opinions (as in the case of empirical evidence) cannot transform other opinions into Platonic knowledge.

31 That segment A is not intended to include also other objects of opinion was argued at length by A.S. Ferguson, 'Plato's simile of light', *Classical Quarterly*, vol. 15, 1921, pp. 131–52, vol. 16, 1922, pp. 15–28, and more recently by Raven, *Plato's Thought in the Making*, Cambridge University Press, 1965, pp. 146–7.

32 Omitting *to* before *ep'*, with Ast (and Cornford?).

33 Thus, Annas, *An Introduction to Plato's Republic*, Oxford, Clarendon Press, 1981, p. 250, must be mistaken when she affirms that 'undoubtedly one function of the Line is to grade our cognitive states according to their distance from full knowledge with understanding'. The Line is not 'a classification of cognitive states and their objects'. Cf. note 19, above.

34 *Parmenides* 129 A5; cf. *Sophist* 259 B–D.

35 Cf. *Meno* 75 B10–11, *Seventh Letter* 342 C6, D4–5, *Phaedrus* 247 C6, *Parmenides* 137 D8. At *Phaedo* 79 A one manuscript has the interesting variant *aeides* ('formless') contrasting with *horaton* ('visible'), instead of the rather more obvious *aides* ('invisible').

36 *Idein . . . idoi tis*, as opposed to the more corporeal *horao*.

37 *Philebus* 39 B classifies imagination alongside memory and sensation, and makes it dependent on 'sight or other sense'.

38 This is not to be construed as special pleading. It is no more than assuming that Plato meant what he said unless proof should be shown of the con-trary. There is no *prima facie* reason to suppose that the intelligible square should have spatial properties when we are expressly told that *noeta* are not spatial entities. I take a kinder view of the Line than does, e.g., Annas, *An Introduction to Plato's Republic*, Oxford, Clarendon

Press, 1981, Ch. 11, with whom, nevertheless, I can go a long way.

39 'Square' here is neither univocal nor equivocal; it is systematically ambiguous, as was recognized, in modern times, already by L. Robin, *La théorie platonicienne des idées et des nombres d'après Aristote*, Paris, Presses Universitaires de France, 1908, repr. Hildesheim, G. Olms, 1963, p. 607. More recent bibliography is supplied by R.A. Shiner, 'Self-predication and the "third man" argument', *Journal of the History of Philosophy*, vol. 8, 1970, pp. 371–86. See also note 16, above.

40 This should not be understood as implying that Plato was on his way to analytical geometry. Our analytical geometry assigns coordinates to places and regards lines as mappings of functions. Plato did not think arithmetic and geometry to be intertranslatable by means of a useful convention; he thought numbered things to be ontologically connected by a common cause to shapes and volumes. And, in any case, the concept of a variable, which is central to analytical geometry, was unknown to him.

41 *Theaetetus* 174 Dff.

42 Cf. *Philebus* 14 D.

43 Plato thought simple numerical relations would explain it. But then he thought intelligibility itself to be a matter of relations.

44 Such was, indeed, Aristotle's view. The *locus classicus* is *Posterior Analytics* I 32.

45 Some such theory was being developed in the Academy, as attested to by the fifth book of Euclid, which is agreed to go back to Platonic circles.

46 The cubic altar in Delos is to be doubled. What is the length of the side of the double cube?

47 Cf. *Euthydemus* 123 D7–10. No doubt, Pythagorean mathematics had much to do with this; cf. D. Ross, *Plato's Theory of Ideas*, Oxford University Press, 1951, p. 49. But other philosophers and mathematicians, like Kant, Brouwer and Beth, came to much the same conclusions, on somewhat different grounds.

48 Cf. *Phaedo* 104 A–105 B.

49 For the Academic definition of number as 'definite plurality' (*plethos peperasmenon*), i.e. a plurality taken as a definite and unified whole, see D. Ross, *Aristotle's Metaphysics*, Oxford, Clarendon Press, 1924, pp. 323–4.

50 Cf. 547 B2ff.

51 The central section of the *Republic*, by explaining the structural nature of the ideas, has shown how soul and city are (structurally) the same, thus giving full support to the analogy of the small and large letters, which was only provisionally accepted as a working hypothesis. Cf. the modalities in 445 C9–10 and in 544 D5–6.

52 On Socrates' view, cf. Ch. 3 in this book. Hierarchy there must be, in the sense that the parts are to be subordinated to the general structure of the

whole. But perhaps there is no need that one of the parts be superordinated to the others, especially in the state. However, for Plato, the structural principle is reason. One could still object to reason in the state being impersonated in one man or in a few men. Rousseau's alternative of having reason distributed all over the state as a whole can lead to consequences no less distasteful – unless reason is denied the power of choosing ends. But we have seen why Plato opposed such a view of reason.

53 There is never full parallelism between Platonic myths. Cf., e.g., the descriptions of the soul or the eschatological myths in the various dialogues. Platonic myths signify, or refer to, some reality, in a special indirect way. See Ch. 12 in this book.

54 But there is a *techne* of the use of psychological means to bring one to the realization of the truth. This is the true rhetoric of *Phaedrus* 270 Bff.

55 Not an uncommon ploy of Plato's. Cf. the cave in *Phaedo* 110 Bff. Plato may have taken the device from Heraclitus. Cf. *Greater Hippias* 289 A–B, quoting Heraclitus, frs 82–3.

56 Cf. pp. 9–10, 48 in this book.

57 Kant could conceive of moral values as imposed on empirical reality. Plato, for reasons explained above (p. 76), could not have a source of values outside reality. Therefore, if he denied that moral values arise from empirical situations, he had to place them in a reality which was in itself non-empirical.

58 As feared by Annas, *An Introduction to Plato's Republic*, Oxford, Clarendon Press, 1981, pp. 264ff.

59 Annas, *An Introduction to Plato's Republic*, Oxford, Clarendon Press, 1981, p. 269.

Chapter 11 Virtue without knowledge: *Republic* I–IV, IX–X

See E. Barker, *Greek Political Theory: Plato and His Predecessors*, London, Methuen, 1918; G. Vlastos (ed.), *Plato*, vol. II, London, Macmillan, 1972; L.G. Versenyi, 'Plato and his liberal opponents', *Philosophy*, vol. 16, 1971, pp. 222–37; J. Neu, 'Plato's analogy of state and individual: the *Republic* and the organic theory of the state', *ibid*., pp. 238–54; R. Barrow, *Plato, Utilitarianism and Education*, London, Routledge & Kegan Paul, 1975; J. Cooper, 'The psychology of justice in Plato', *American Philosophical Quarterly*, 1977; G.R. Morrow, 'Plato's concept of persuasion', *Philosophical Review*, vol. 62, 1953, pp. 234–50; K. Dover, *Greek Popular Morality in the Time of Plato and Aristotle*, Berkeley, University of California Press, 1974; J. Annas, *An Introduction to Plato's Republic*, Oxford, Clarendon Press, 1981.

1 Thrasymachus: 336 B–344 A; Glaucon's 'social contract': 358 B–359 B; Gyges' ring: 359 B–360 D, cf. also Antiphon, fr. 44 A and p. 10 in this book.

2 On conflict within the individual, see, on the *Gorgias*, pp. 40f., and p. 102f. in this book.

3 Political theory deals with the limitations imposed on one's activities by the presence of other agents with their own interests. Of course, there are other types of limitations, imposed by the natural environment, by one's psychological make-up, by one's own moral or religious convictions, etc. But these, at least initially, do not fall within the domain of political theory. It will be part of the underlying assumptions of Plato's argument that politics cannot be separated from these other aspects.

4 Lycophron and Hippodamus (pp. 10–11 in this book) thought it was, as did all liberal thinkers in general, as well as some modern commentators of Plato. Cf., e.g., W.A.R. Leys, 'Was Plato non-political?' and F.E. Sparshott, 'Plato as non-political thinker', in Vlastos (ed.), *Plato*, vol. II, London, Macmillan, pp. 16–86, answered by J.B. Skemp, 'How political is the *Republic*?', *History of Political Thought*, 1, 1980, pp. 1–7. Modern liberal political thought tends to take consensus almost for granted – possibly because historically it is a development of the national state.

5 Skemp, 'How political is the *Republic*?', *History of Political Thought*, 1, 1980, p. 2. For the modern controversy over liberalism, see M.J. Sandel (ed.), *Liberalism and Its Critics*, New York, New York University Press, 1984. Plato too, as the modern communitarians, maintained that man's deepest interests are not independent of society. But unlike them, Plato does not consider socially dependent interests as defined within the social framework but only as an expression of interests which are transcendent. This is clear, e.g., from *Symposium* 211–12, where laws and social arrangements are only rungs in the scale of the beautiful.

6 Cf. Ch. 9 in this book.

7 The soul, 'in its true form', is one – see *Republic* 611 B9. Cf. W.K.C. Guthrie, 'Plato's views on the nature of the soul', *Recherches sur la tradition platonicienne, Entretiens*, vol. III, Vandoeuvres-Genève, Fondation Hardt, pp. 2–19, repr. in G. Vlastos (ed.), *Plato*, vol. II, London, Macmillan, 1972, pp. 230–43; J. Moline, 'Plato on the Complexity of the Psyche', *Archiv für Geschichte der Philosophie*, vol. 60, 1978, pp. 1–26; and my 'Reason and Passion in the Platonic Soul', *Dionysius*, vol. 2, 1978, pp. 35–48.

8 On the education of the emotions, see R.F. Dearden, P.H. Hirst and R.S. Peters (eds), *Education and the Development of Reason*, London, Routledge & Kegan Paul, 1972.

9 Annas, *An Introduction to Plato's Republic*, Oxford, Clarendon Press, 1981, p. 91.

10 Cf., e.g., *Theaetetus* 151 A–B.

11 Cf. pp. 18–19 in this book.

12 At this stage, Plato does not yet distinguish between propositions and concepts. He will do it explicitly at *Sophist* 261 Cff.

13 B. Campbell, 'Intellect and the political order in Plato's *Republic*', *History of Political Thought*, vol. 1, 1980, p. 389.

14 *Mousike* includes all the arts and letters. Plato's main interest is in poetry (which was mostly sung) and drama, but he discusses also instrumental music, dance, painting and sculpture.

15 Cf. G.M.A. Grube, *Plato's Thought*, London, Methuen, 1935 (Boston, Beacon Press, 1958), pp. 251–2.

16 As young Charmides, in the dialogue, called after him.

17 On the development of moral reasoning from unconscious habits, see, e.g., R.M. Hare, 'Adolescents into adults', in T.H.B. Hollins (ed.), *Aims in Education*, Manchester University Press, 1964, pp. 47–70. But Plato would maintain, against Hare, that moral reasoning cannot be purely formal.

18 Fr. 41. E. Diehl, *Anthologia Lyrica Graeca*, 3rd ed., vol. I, Leipzig, Teubner, 1949–52.

19 'Righteousness' would perhaps be a more accurate translation of *dikaiosune*. But, in the present context, the traditional translation keeps the political implications of *dikaiosune*.

20 On justice as mental health, see Kenny, in n. 36 to Ch. 5 of this book, and R.F. Stalley, 'Mental health and individual responsibility in Plato's *Republic*', *Journal of Value Inquiry*, vol. 15, 1981, pp. 109–24.

21 Cf. G. Klosko, '*Demotike arete* in the *Republic*', *History of Political Thought*, 3, 1982, pp. 363–82, and bibliographical notes there. The phrase is Butler's, quoted by Klosko at p. 371 n. 18.

22 Cf. pp. 27–8 in this book.

23 Klosko, '*Demotike arete* in the *Republic*', *History of Political Thought*, 3, 1982, p. 378, gives the examples of the cigarette smoker and the drug addict. Cf. Protagoras' view, p. 7 in this book.

24 On popular ('demotic') virtue, see Annas, *An Introduction to Plato's Republic*, Oxford, Clarendon Press, 1981, Ch. 5, and Klosko, '*Demotike arete* in the *Republic*', *History of Political Thought*, 3, 1982, pp. 363–82, against R. Kraut, 'Reason and justice in Plato's *Republic*' in E.N. Lee, A.D.P. Mourelatos and R.M. Rorty, (eds), *Exegesis and Argument*, Assen, Van Gorcum, 1973, pp. 207–24. For a contemporary version of the debate over instrumental reason, cf. B. Williams, *Problems of the Self*, Cambridge University Press, 1973, and T. Nagel, *The View from Nowhere*, Oxford University Press, 1986.

25 The problem is discussed aporetically in the *Euthyphro*.

26 Cf. *Meno* 97 Dff.

27 Annas, *An Introduction to Plato's Republic*, Oxford, Clarendon Press, 1981, p. 86. But doesn't the concept of moral stages imply that some people's morals are better than others? Cf., e.g., L. Kohlberg, 'Education for justice: a Platonic view', in T.R. Sizer (ed.), *Moral Education*, Cambridge, Mass., Harvard University Press, 1970, pp. 55–83. Kohlberg,

however, is hardly Platonic. There is in Kohlberg's stages no clarification of emotions (not of values!) and there is no logical progression from one state to the next. Moreover, it is Plato's firm conviction, against Protagoras, that conflicting moral systems cannot all be coherent. This is the lesson of the central similes of the *Republic*, and this is why Plato denies that ethics can be separated from ontology.

28 Cf. *Gorgias* 454 C7ff.

29 As R. Martin, 'The ideal state in Plato's *Republic*', *History of Political Thought*, vol. 2, 1981, pp. 1–30, thinks. But he misunderstands the hermeneutical status of the final myth.

30 On the *Statesman* (or *Politicus*), see *Plato's Statesman*, tr. with introduction and notes by J.B. Skemp, London, Routledge & Kegan Paul, 1952.

31 Not unlike the (admittedly more restricted) power of pardon given to the Queen or the President.

32 Rationality implies absolute primacy of the law if reason is conceived as the faculty concerned with general rules, as in Kant or Hegel. But Plato's reason (*nous*) is concerned with giving of reasons (*logoi*), not with establishing laws.

Chapter 12 An educator looks at literature and drama: *Republic* II–III, X

See J. Tate, ' "Imitation" in Plato's *Republic*', *Classical Quarterly*, vol. 22, 1928, pp. 16–23; and 'Plato and "Imitation" ', *Classical Quarterly*, vol. 26, 1932, pp. 161–70; M.J. Verdenius, *Mimesis: Plato's Doctrine of Artistic Imitation*, Leiden, E.J. Brill, 1949; C.L. Griswold, 'The ideas and the criticism of poetry in Plato's *Republic* Book X', *Journal of the History of Philosophy*, vol. 19, 1981, pp. 135–50; J. Moravcsik and P. Temko (eds), *Plato on Beauty, Wisdom and the Arts*, *American Philosophical Quarterly* monograph, Pittsburgh, 1982; J.A. Stewart, *The Myths of Plato*, London, Macmillan, 1905; P. Frutiger, *Les mythes de Platon*, Paris, F. Alcan, 1930; L. Edelstein, 'The function of myth in Plato's philosophy', *Journal of the History of Ideas*, vol. 10, 1949, pp. 463–81; G.D. Stromer, 'Plato's theory of myth', *The Personalist*, vol. 55, 1974, pp. 216–33. See also F.E. Sparshott, 'The truth about gods and men', *Dialogue*, vol. 10, 1970, pp. 3–11.

1 Cf. pp. 78–9 in this book. On cognitive emotions, cf. I. Scheffler, 'In praise of cognitive emotions', *Teachers College Record*, 79, 1977, pp. 171–86. See also A.O. Rorty (ed.), *Explaining Emotions*, Berkeley, University of California Press, 1980; R.F. Dearden, P.H. Hirst and R.S. Peters (eds), *Education and the Development of Reason*, London, Routledge & Kegan Paul, 1972.

2 On painting, cf. 595 A–598 D; on music and dance, cf. *Republic* 398 C–

400 C, and W.D. Anderson, *Ethos and Education in Greek Music*, Cambridge, Mass., Harvard University Press, 1960, Ch. III.

3 Cf. *Laws* 669 A7–B3.

4 For a critique of the 'aesthetic consciousness', see H.-G. Gadamer, 'Plato and the poets' (1934), *Dialogue and Dialectic: Eight Hermeneutical Studies on Plato*, tr. P. Christopher Smith, New Haven and London, Yale University Press, 1980.

5 On Plato's own dialogues, cf. pp. 116–19 in this book. I owe the clarification of this point, and many other good things in this chapter, to my wife, Hanna.

6 For different perspectives on art and literature, cf., e.g., the *Ion* and especially the *Phaedrus*.

7 Apparently, Plato himself was not much concerned with violence as such, although there is hardly a bloodless page in the *Iliad*.

8 Cf., e.g., *Phaedrus* 252 Cff.

9 Cf. *Phaedrus* 229 C6ff.

10 On myth as expressing the general by means of the particular, see E. Cassirer, *The Philosophy of Symbolic Forms*, tr. R. Manheim, New Haven and London, Yale University Press, 1955, Ch. 1.

11 Cf. Pausanias I 20 3; *Iliad* I 586–94.

12 This is not to say that Plato did not believe in reincarnation. He expressly says he trusts the myth to be true (81 E1–2 *ho ego pisteuon alethei einai*). But he commends its acceptance on the force of its moral consequences, not on the force of his belief in it.

13 *Pseudos*: not necessarily 'lie'. Cornford suggests 'fiction', in some contexts.

14 God is truthful and undeceptive. Were he not so, there would be no guarantee that we have knowledge of reality. Cf. p. 90 in this book. For a self-conscious Romantic alternative to the Greek ideal of immutability, cf., e.g. Goethe's 'Four Seasons': 'Warum bin ich vergänglich, o Zeus? so fragte die Schönheit./Macht ich doch, sagte der Gott, nur das Vergängliche schön.' ('Why am I ephemeral, Zeus? so Beauty asked him./Yet I made, said the god, only the ephemeral beautiful.')

15 *Homoiosis*, 'being made like', not *mimesis*, which is sometimes better translated as 'representation'.

16 Plato's philosophical hero is, of course, Socrates. Alcibiades in his speech in the *Symposium* (215 A–222 B) ascribes to him all four traditional virtues.

17 *Gorgias* 470 C9–471 D2.

18 The likely or the probable (Aristotle's *eikos*, *Poetics* 9. 1451 a38ff.) is an empirical category no less than the factual.

19 For a perceptive analysis of Plato's criticism of tragedy, cf. V. Goldschmidt, 'Le problème de la tragédie d'après Platon', *Questions platoniciennes*, Paris, J. Vrin, 1970, pp. 103–40.

20 Cf. *Laws* 817 Aff.; Aristotle, *Poetics* 6. 1449 b24.
21 Cf. p. 34 in this book.
22 Cf. Aristotle, *Nicomachean Ethics* II 9.
23 Cf. *Phaedo* 89 A–C, in the almost exact middle of the dialogue, and the exchange with Crito towards its end, at 115 B.
24 *Hupolepteon*, the technical verb for assuming a *hupothesis*.
25 *E kai*; cf. J.D. Denniston, *The Greek Particles*, 2nd ed., Oxford, Clarendon Press, 1954, p. 306.
26 *Republic* 359 C (cf. p. 101 in this book), referred back to at 612 B.

Index